1/26/93

the Name of the game
of the
How Sports Talk Got That Way

Lafe Locke

D1569085

BETTERWAY PUBLICATIONS, INC.
WHITE HALL, VIRGINIA

Other books by Lafe Locke:

Film Animation Techniques
Exploring Advertising Design
Adventures in Advertising
Card Sense & Nonsense

Published by Betterway Publications, Inc.
P.O. Box 219
Crozet, VA 22932
(804) 823-5661

Cover design by Susan Riley
Drawings by Lafe Locke
Typography by Blackhawk Typesetting

Library of Congress Cataloging-in-Publication Data
Locke, Lafe
    The name of the game : how sports talk got that way / Lafe Locke.
        p. cm.
    Includes index.
    Summary: Explains the origins and derivations of words and phrases in over twenty-five sports, relating them to the development of the sports themselves.
    ISBN 1-55870-234-2 : $7.95
    1. Sports—Miscellanea—Juvenile literature. 2. Sports — Terminology—Juvenile literature. [1. Sports—Terminology. 2. Sports—Miscellanea.] I. Title.
GV706.8.L63 1992
796—dc20   91-43799
                                                                              CIP
                                                                               AC
Printed in the United States of America
0 9 8 7 6 5 4 3 2 1

Acknowledgments

This book is right off the wall. The inspiration for it is a series of twenty posters used in high school physical education programs. The posters were designed and written by myself and issued by J. Weston Walch, educational publisher in Portland, Maine. I wish to thank Walch editors Jane Carter and Rick Kimball, who encouraged me to expand the poster material into this book for your information and enjoyment.

Contents

Introduction

Did you know the word *gymnastics* comes from an old Greek word *gymna-zein*? It means "to exercise naked." Or that hockey got its name from the Indian equivalent of "Ouch!"? They were really yelling *ho ghee*, which means "It hurts!" Try it the next time you catch a slap shot in the solar plexus.

At least that's the latest scoop on how two popular sports came to be named. There are other versions, of course, and you'll read about them in this book, along with information about *le jeu de paume* (tennis), *game of fives* (handball), *peach ball* (basketball), *baggataway* (lacrosse), *harpastum* (soccer), and even the tongue-twister *schweitzer schwingen* (a "schwinging" style of Swiss wrestling).

Whether you participate or just watch, sports and games are a lot more fun if you know something about how they came to be and how they got their names. This book gives you facts, theories, and some just plain guesses about the origins of the names of over two dozen of them. There are tales of how the games originated and developed, too, because in most cases the way a game is played or the equipment that is used has a bearing on what the sport is called. For instance, you'll learn the real reason why basketball players are often called "cagers" and why we say "love" instead of "zero" when scoring tennis.

You also may be surprised to learn that assorted kings, queens, and emperors tried to blow the whistle on the most popular sports because they either interfered with military training or were considered "too gentle" to help soldiers shape up for war.

Incidentally, as a sports fan you might be interested to know that *fan* was coined in 1883 by Ted Sullivan, manager of the St. Louis Browns, as a quicker way of saying *fanatic*. Back when that word fanatic first cropped up it didn't have anything to do with sports. It's from Latin and means to be "inspired by a divinity."

Winston Churchill, the British statesman, had another idea. He said a fanatic is a person "who can't change his mind and won't change the subject."

Maybe you know some sports fans (or fanatics) who claim they're the only ones who know the score. So give your curiosity a workout and read on. You could be the sage of the locker room or the sharpest sports commentator on your block.

1

The Olympic Games
The Thirty-Second Send-Off

Pity the spectator who dropped his program at the first Olympic Game. As he stooped to pick it up, he probably missed the main event. It was a foot race lasting less than thirty seconds! And it was the *only* athletic event of the day because that original race at Olympia, Greece in 776 B.C. was part of a big religious ceremony held in honor of Zeus, the top-ranked Greek god.

The winner of the race, Coroebus, was a cook from the nearby town of Elis, and thus became the very first Olympic champion. He and several other runners sprinted naked (a custom at the time) on a sandy track 630 feet long. The distance was a Greek measure called a *stade*, from which we get our modern word *stadium*.

Why was a foot race at a religious ceremony? Next to their many gods and goddesses, the ancient Greeks revered athletic skill above all things. They reasoned that the best way to honor the gods was to develop discipline in body and mind. Since a big festival and ceremony were held for Zeus every four years at Olympia, somebody got the idea of staging a race with the fastest sprinters from several towns and cities in the running.

No need telling you that the idea caught on like hot dogs and ice cream. As years passed, more athletic events were added. The original foot race in which Coroebus won himself a crown of laurel leaves became known as the *Olympic Games*, and cities all over Greece sent their best athletes there to "win their laurels," too. Eventually the athletic activities became more important than the ceremony for Zeus as thousands of spectators jammed into the stadium to cheer their favorites.

Don't get the idea that the Olympic Games were named for *Olympia*, the town where the games were first held, or even for *Mount Olympus*, the mythical home of the gods, which is several hundred miles away. The name comes from the Greek word *olympiad*, which stands for a period of time spanning four years. The festivals to Zeus and the athletic games that were to make them even more popular were held every four years at a site selected for Zeus's temple in a beautiful valley beside a winding river. It is possible the town that grew up there got its name from the olympiad instead of the other way around. In any event, the custom of holding the games every four years is still followed in the modern Olympic Games.

There are several conflicting tales about the beginning of the festivals that led to the Olympic Games. They go back thousands of years before Coroebus won his wreath in that first official foot race in 776 B.C. But once the Games were established (see the next chapter), they were repeated every four years for the next 1,200 years. At first, only a few nearby towns got in the act. But the popularity—and rivalry for Olympic laurels—soon spread across Greece, and from there to other lands and islands such as Rhodes, Crete, Sicily, Egypt, and Asia Minor. More athletic events were introduced into the Games as participation grew.

Coroebus, a fast foods cook from Elis, won the first Olympic race.

The Games not only served as a common link among the peoples around the eastern rim of the Mediterranean Sea, they also helped promote peace. At the time the Games were started, there were practically no large nations as we know them today. Just about every town and city was an independent city-state and jealous of its neighbors. There was a lot of bickering, which often led to war.

Despite this rivalry, everybody wanted to make a good showing at the temple of Zeus every four years and carry off the Olympic laurels. It was better to beat rival cities in races and boxing matches than to clobber them with swords and spears. Thus, there was a relatively peaceful period every time the Games were held. Fighting usually stopped as warriors went to show off their skills in more peaceful competitions. And in many instances, the wars didn't resume when the Games were over. Too bad this wasn't the case during World War I and World War II, when the Olympic Games were suspended instead of the battles.

There were many notable champions in the early Olympic Games, particularly those who won their events again and again over the years. One standout was Milo of Croton, who won the wrestling championship six times during the sixth century B.C. He was known for many feats of strength, but the main reason Milo is remembered is the way he developed that tremendous strength. According to legend, he's the fellow who hoisted a calf onto his shoulders every day until the calf was a full-grown bull. Try it, if you've got the calf and the time.

Eventually the Games at Olympia did come to an end. The Romans conquered Greece in 146 B.C. and continued to hold athletic competitions there for a few more centuries, but the Games began to go downhill. One story tells us that the Roman emperor Nero himself entered some of the events, but intimidated his opponents to gain an advantage. In one instance, he entered a chariot race while drunk. No one would compete against him, and even though he fell out of his chariot and couldn't finish the race, he was declared the winner. Emperors can get away with that sort of thing, it seems.

Finally, in 393 A.D., Emperor Theodosius I, who had been converted to Christianity, blew the whistle on the Games because, he said, they were pagan activities and a "public nuisance." Even the "eternal flame" in the Temple of Zeus was put out, and the Olympic stadium and surrounding buildings were either torn down or left to destruction by floods and earthquakes. It took fifteen centuries to get the Olympic Games going again.

April 6, 1896 is the date of the start of the modern Olympic Games. It happened in Athens, Greece, but the man most responsible for the revival of the Games was a go-ahead French baron named Pierre de Coubertin. Though only five feet, three inches tall and not an athlete himself, Coubertin nevertheless managed almost single-handedly to promote the idea of an international amateur athletic competition patterned after the original Olympics. In a meeting of representatives from nine nations, held in Paris, his idea was accepted and Athens was chosen as the place to renew the Games.

Right away there was a snag in the plan. Athens was only too happy to be host to the modern Olympics, but the city wasn't prepared for the job. There was a stadium, for sure. But it had been built in 143 B.C. and wasn't in too great shape after more than a thousand years. Just when fund-raising efforts looked like they would fail, George Averoff, a wealthy Greek merchant who lived in Alexandria, Egypt, declared he would foot the entire bill for reconstruction of the stone and marble stadium. It cost him a million drachmas, and the Olympics went on as scheduled!

Compared to today's Games, the first modern Olympics in 1896 wouldn't make much of a show. Only 311 athletes from thirteen nations were entered. Compare that with the more than 8,000 athletes from about 140 countries who show up for the summer and winter Olympics these days. There were forty events in the 1896 program. The thirteen-man United States squad captured first place with eleven gold medals, seven silver, and a bronze. Greece won second place, and Germany took third.

One name in the American group is worth remembering. He was James B. Connolly, a freshman at Harvard and an outstanding jumper. When the Harvard dean wouldn't give Connolly permission to attend the Olympics, he dropped out of school and went anyway, paying his own expenses. Later Harvard was pleased as punch that Connolly had defied the dean. He won a gold medal in the triple jump event (hop, step, and jump), leaping forty-five feet. What's more, since it was the first event to be completed at the meet, Connolly became the first modern Olympic Gold Medalist. Thus, he goes into memory along with Coroebus, the cook who won the very first Olympic laurels in 776 B.C.

Many thousands of Olympic medals have been won since that great day in Athens near the turn of this century. And some of the medal winners took their fame and their good looks to Hollywood, where they became better known as movie stars. There was Duke Kahanamoku, a Hawaiian, the first person on record to swim 100 meters in less than a minute. He appeared in several Hollywood films. Johnny Weissmuller took over from Duke to win five gold medals in Olympic swimming events, but you know him better for his screen role as Tarzan of the Apes. Another Olympic swimming champion who later beat his chest and said, "Me Tarzan, you Jane," was Clarence "Buster" Crabbe. He also played Flash Gordon and Buck Rogers. Aileen Riggin, a diving champion, and Eleanor Holm, backstroke medalist, also took their fame and beauty to the Hollywood screen.

The variety and quality of Olympic competition have grown as more and more nations joined in. Records by the score have been broken and re-broken. The first winter sport, figure skating, was introduced in London in 1908, and Olympic Winter Games were begun as a separate competition at Chamonix, France in 1914.

Women — six tennis players — first competed in the Olympics in 1900. Charlotte Cooper of Great Britain became the first-ever female Gold Medalist by winning at lawn tennis singles. But wait! There's more about the girls in the next chapter. Listen up, fellows.

Milo of Croton was adept at wrestling and slinging the bull.

2

The Girls Join In

We Can Do Anything Better than You

There never was a Ladies' Day at the ancient Olympic Games. And as far as it is known, only one woman ever got to see them. Females were strictly barred from the competition, and, to add to the insult, the Game officials wouldn't even let women inside the stadium as spectators. The rule was so strictly enforced that any female caught climbing a tree outside the stadium to get a glimpse inside was promptly put to death by tossing her over a cliff. Those ancient Greeks played rough.

However, 380 years after the start of the Games, a woman actually did get inside the stadium to see what was going on — and lived to tell about it. She was a widow from the Island of Rhodes and her name was *Kallipateira*. (Some legends say her name was *Pherenice*.) The lady had a good reason for getting in. She wanted to help with the training of her son, who was competing in the boxing matches. So Mrs. K (or maybe Mrs. P) dressed as a man and walked boldly through the arched entrance to the stadium. But when her son won his match, Mom gave herself away by hugging and kissing him. She escaped being put to death only because her father, Diagoras, had been a celebrated Olympic boxing champion some years before. The officials just tossed her out instead of over a cliff, and to avoid any more male-female mix-ups in the future they ruled that all trainers would have to appear naked at the Games.

Of course, a lot of girls and women resented being kept out of the Olympic Games. So they did the next best thing and started holding contests of their own. One girl in particular, a beautiful Greek princess named Hippodameia, did it up in style.

The name *Hippodameia*, incidentally, is a combination of Greek words that have nothing to do with a good-looking princess. The name means "a place for horse racing." That's where our modern word *hippodrome* comes from.

Hippodameia's father probably gave her that name because he liked fast horses, as may be seen in the legend of the beginning of the male Olympics. Hippodameia was partly responsible for that, too. As was mentioned earlier, there are several tales about how the Games got started. But this most-told tale says an oracle told Hippodameia's father, King Oenomaus, that he would be slain by his son-in-law. The king wasn't about to let that happen, so he got himself the fastest chariot horses available. Then he let it be known that any young fellow who wanted to marry his daughter would first have to take her from home by chariot and outrace him when he chased after them. A winner could marry the princess, but woe to the loser. The king also said every loser in the race would be slain. (We already said those old Greeks played rough.)

No less than thirteen suitors tried for Hippodameia's hand … and died in the attempt. The king's horses were too fast for them, and he killed each suitor with a spear as he raced past him.

Then along came a handsome bachelor named Pelops. He knew something about chariot racing and also knew how to fix the odds in his favor. Pelops bribed a stableman to remove a metal pin that held one of the wheels to King Oenomaus's chariot. The wheel came off during the race. The king was killed. And Pelops won the race, the bride, and the kingdom.

To celebrate his victory, the legend continues, Pelops organized the first Olympic Game, which, as you've already learned, was a foot race won by Coroebus, a cook from Elis.

You'd think that Hippodameia, being the new bride of the founder of the Games, would at least have been given a free pass for a seat in the bleachers. But instead, the "Females Keep Out" sign went up. She retaliated by organizing a female olympiad of her own. She got several girlfriends together for the first of a long series of *Heraea*, that is, athletic events for women only. They were named after Hera, the wife of Zeus, who also had a temple at Olympia.

Like the Olympic Games, the Heraea were held every four years. But they were sandwiched in between the Olympics to avoid conflicting dates. At first, Hippodameia invited only a circle

Until the 1800s, sporting women were considered "unladylike."

of her friends to compete and be spectators. But soon women from all over Greece were invited to take part and many more came just to watch and cheer their favorites.

You guessed it, no men were allowed at the Heraea, even though the bars may have been lowered for female spectators at the male Olympics some time later. Some historians believe the incident in which Kallipateira was caught in the stadium masquerading as a man shook up the stadium officials to a point that they started admitting women. There is no convincing record of this, however.

Another belief that is subject to speculation is that the women's games, the Heraea, were suspended shortly after the Romans conquered Greece in 146 B.C. This claim is based on the lack of any record of female games after that time. But there are some sketchy tales that indicate women may have been allowed to compete with men in chariot races.

Centuries later, women athletes finally became accepted Olympic competitors. It was in 1900 when the second meeting of the modern Olympic Games was held in Paris. There Charlotte Cooper of Great Britain won the women's title in lawn tennis singles and became the first female Gold Medalist in history.

Women from the United States didn't enter Olympic competition until 1920. That year a small team went to Antwerp, Belgium and captured first place in four of the five women's swimming and diving events.

In the more than 900 years the ancient Greek Heraea were in action, there surely were some outstanding women athletes. But they got very poor press and we know next to nothing about them. The early Greek chroniclers spent their time telling of the daring deeds of the male contestants at Olympia. For that reason, plus the suspension of all the Games for several centuries, women in sports didn't get much notice in the history books until the fourteenth century when Queen Elizabeth I of England is said to have enjoyed hunting and watching dog races. But she may not have scored very high among sports fans since she banned the playing of football. She said it kept too many men from practicing archery, something they needed when in the army.

Then, in the sixteenth century, there was Mary, Queen of Scots. She is said to be the first woman to get hooked on golf. About 150 years later, Queen Anne of England was a great fan of horse racing, but you wouldn't call her an athlete. She got so fat she had to be carried up and down the palace stairs.

In fact, for many centuries the idea of females taking part in physical sports was frowned on. The word had gotten around that running, jumping, and the like weren't "ladylike." But, like Hippodameia and her girlfriends back in ancient times, modern women began to flex their muscles in the 1800s. First, it was considered okay to engage in archery and croquet. Then more of the girls went in for golf and some tried swimming. As we will see later on, it was a young woman who brought tennis to America in 1874, though female members of royalty in France and England had played the game for many years before that.

Today there are so many young women who have made names for themselves in the sports record books it would be hard to single out the very best. But we ought to mention a few because they excelled in many sports and not only broke records, they broke down barriers against women athletes.

A pioneer among them was Lottie Dod of England. Beginning in 1887 when she was only fifteen years old, Miss Dod won five tennis singles championships at Wimbledon. Then she took the British women's golf title and went on to win tournaments in field hockey and archery. She also showed what women could do by passing an ice skating test in Switzerland that had been prepared strictly for male experts.

Lottie's winning a championship at age fifteen isn't so unusual. Aileen Riggin, a member of that first women's U.S. Olympic team in 1920, was only fourteen when she took a Gold Medal in springboard diving. Sonja Henie was just ten years old and already the figure skating champion of Norway when she entered the Olympic Winter Games in 1924. She placed last, but came back four years later — all five feet and 100 pounds of her — to win the first of three consecutive Gold Medals. Tracy Caulkins of the United States was fifteen when she won five Gold Medals and a Silver at a single World Championship swim meet at West Berlin in 1978, a non-Olympiad year. Tracy also won forty-eight national swim titles, twelve more than Johnny "Tarzan" Weissmuller. There have been numerous eleven- and twelve-year-old girls who have won Silver and Bronze Olympic medals or made very good showings against international competition.

Mary Queen of Scots was the first woman hooked on golf.

Eleanora Sears, a Boston socialite, was another woman who made sports page headlines. Around the turn of this century, Miss Sears made her mark, or marks, in golf, tennis, canoeing, sailing, swimming, hiking, horseback riding, and rifle shooting. After creating a ruckus in England by entering a men's polo match wearing trousers just like the men players wore, she went on to challenge other males to beat her in auto and speed boat racing. There were no takers. In 1934, at age fifty, Miss Sears won the U.S. squash singles championship.

A Champion of Champions award should also go to another American and all-round athlete, Mrs. Mildred (Babe) Didrikson Zaharias. Hometown folks in Beaumont, Texas called her Babe because the tomboy kid could swat a baseball almost as far as the real Babe Ruth could. She began her sports career in basketball, but collected medals and other laurels in a wide variety of sports. Babe is probably best remembered for her exploits as a professional golfer, though her list of amateur athletic feats is as long as your arm. For example, she broke the world record for the high jump at the 1932 Olympic Games in Los Angeles.

The Encyclopedia of Sports says Babe Didrikson entered 634 amateur competitions and won 632 of them! Top that, you guys!

3

Aquatics
Everybody's in the Swim

Our word *aquatics*, which comes from the Latin word *aqua*, meaning "water," is a fancy way of saying *water sports*. It covers a number of individual and team sports, particularly swimming, and uncounted centuries of activity in water.

SWIMMING

Primitive legends, hieroglyphic symbols, ancient sculptures, and even the Bible testify to man's early ability to swim, dive, and row a boat. In the ancient picture writing of Egypt, for example, the sign for "swim" was a man's head with one arm reaching forward and the other back. Even then, in times when the pyramids were being built, they knew about the "crawl" stroke that modern swimmers use for speed.

We know the ancient Greeks were swimmers because of the famous legend of Leander and Hero. She lived on one side of the Hellespont, an arm of the sea now called the Dardanelles, and Leander lived on the other shore. The distance was either two or four miles, according to where historians think Leander took the plunge. The pair were in love, so every evening Leander swam across the Hellespont to see Hero, and swam back in the morning. It was a tough way to keep a steady date. So tough, in fact, that on one crossing Leander was drowned. Tearful Hero drowned herself, too.

Centuries later in 1810, Lord Byron, the famed English romantic poet, repeated the swim across the Dardanelles. But knowing what happened to Leander, Lord Byron hedged his bet by having a Lieutenant Ekenhead swim along with him. They made the crossing in one hour and ten minutes, not a bad pace for a beginner — and a poet at that.

Who was the first swimmer? Nobody knows, of course, because it probably was some early cave man who didn't watch his step and accidentally fell into a lake or river. He had to dog-paddle his way to shore just as he had seen certain animals do. It was a simple case of sink or swim.

Early man learned to swim — or else.

Our word *swim*, which was first used about the middle of the sixteenth century, is a shorter version of the Old English word *swimman*, which means the same thing — to move along in water. And *that* old word is believed to have its root in an Indo-European word, *swem*, also meaning "to move the body along in or on water." Wherever it came from, the word *swim* is used a lot in our language to say things like: "she's in the swim," "she makes my head swim," and "he's swimming against the tide."

We've already mentioned the stumbling cave man who had to "sink or swim." That's a phrase that cropped up all too often back when folks in Europe believed in — and feared — witchcraft. If they suspected a neighbor of being a witch, she was tossed into the nearest pond to sink or swim. If she sank and drowned, she was innocent. If she could swim ashore, it meant she was in league with the devil and was punished accordingly. Either way, sink or swim was a no-win proposition. But let's get back to water sports that are more fun.

Just as the word *swim* has a fairly clear meaning in water sports, the names that have been given to the various types of swimming and diving are easy to understand, too. That's because they describe just what is going on. *Dog-paddle*, for instance; not much argument as to where that term came from. Or *frog kick*, another swimming stroke copied from animal life. And how about *swan dive*, perhaps the most graceful way you can plunge into a pool. *Scissors kick* is another term that is self-explanatory.

The ancients probably used the dog-paddle stroke most often when they wanted to swim, or had to. Mosaic pictures in Pompeii, the Roman city destroyed in an eruption of Mount Vesuvius, show men moving in water by making strokes that look like the dog-paddle.

The English were first to turn swimming into a competitive sport. To get more speed and distance, they developed the *breast stroke* and *side stroke*, and stuck to those methods of swimming until near the end of the 1800s. Nobody seemed to remember that the Egyptians had foretold a better way. Nor did they seem to care that Indians in North and South America and natives of West Africa and the South Pacific islands were swimming with overhand strokes that got them through the water a lot faster than any European could manage.

Even a demonstration as early as 1844 failed to convince European swimmers. In that year, some North American Indians were taken to London to show off their swimming style. They swam the length of a 130-foot pool in thirty seconds by using a form of what we now call the *crawl stroke* and *flutter kick*. But the British only laughed at the feat. A London newspaper described the swimming style as "totally un-European" and said the Indians "thrashed the water violently with their arms, like the sails of a windmill, and beat downward with their feet, blowing with force and performing grotesque antics." The Europeans went right on breast stroking and side stroking for another twenty years or more.

Then, in 1860 or 1880 or 1890, according to which historian you want to believe, an English swimmer and coach was converted to the Indians' way of swimming. He was J. Arthur Trudgen and he had observed the way natives in South America used an overhand stroke while swimming. He introduced the stroke when coaching back in England. It was tried and accepted — and given the name *Trudgen stroke*.

Another Englishman liked the Indian way of swimming, too. His name was Frederick Cavill, a man who took his skill to

Australia in 1878. There he built swimming tanks and, with six sons, had a whole family involved in teaching and competition. The Cavills also copied the way South Pacific islanders used a double overhand stroke together with a downward kick. The Aussies called that way of swimming the *splash stroke.*

Improving on both the overhand stroke and what was to become the *scissors kick,* the Cavills soon were beating all the competition Down Under. Asked to describe his swimming method, one of the Cavill boys said, "It's like crawling through water." And that is how the *crawl stroke* first got its name. As the popularity of the method spread around the world, it became known as the *Australian crawl.* Richard Cavill, the eldest son of the family, went to England in 1902 and set a new speed mark using the Australian crawl. He defeated every swimmer there who was using the Trudgen method, which relied less on leg strokes.

If any of the Cavills were ever entered in Olympic swimming competition, there is no record of it, though the modern Olympics were begun just at the time when the family was becoming famous in Australia. The Cavills aside, when Olympic swimming was revived in Athens in 1896, the races were a far cry from swimming meets held today. There was no regulation pool with water at a controlled temperature. There weren't any firm starting blocks or marked lanes or sophisticated timing devices.

Instead, it was more like a swimming contest at a seaside clambake, except that it was in April and too chilly for picnics. The Olympic swimmers were taken by launch into the Bay of Zea near Athens. The launch was stopped offshore at what was judged to be the right distance for each race. The swimmers jumped into the ice-cold water and a starting gun was fired. First man to the beach was the winner. There were only three races — 100, 500, and 1,500 meters. All were freestyle, and a Hungarian named Alfred Hajos won the shortest and the longest of them. Paul Neumann of Austria won the 500 meter swim.

The next few Olympiads didn't see much improvement in swimming conditions. At Paris four years later, the competitors swam in the Seine River. At least they were allowed to swim downstream with the current. Olympic swimmers also competed in an artificial lake and in a sheltered harbor. A pool was provided in London in 1908, but not until 1912 in Berlin was there a pool with lanes marked with floating ropes.

The unquestioned swimming star of the Olympics to date is

Mark Spitz of the United States. In 1968 and 1972, he won nine Gold Medals and one Silver. World records were broken in seven of the wins. When women's swimming events were first included in the Olympics in 1912, Australia's Fanny Durack became the first female Gold Medalist in water sports. She captured the 100 meter freestyle event. Another female swimming feat should be remembered. On August 11, 1965, not an Olympic year, an American girl, Karen Muir, broke the world backstroke record. Karen was twelve years old and the youngest person ever to hold a world record in a major sport.

A non-Olympic event in which many swimmers excel is *endurance swimming*. They go for distance or time in the water, and it's a grueling sport at best. The world's most famous and frequent of the endurance swims is crossing the English Channel. Since the first successful crossing in 1875, scores of men and women have made the swim, as many as eighteen in a year. Some swimmers cross several times. Many fail in the attempt, too, because the distance measured on a map can be misleading. It's twenty miles. But, because of strong tides and treacherous currents in the English Channel, many swimmers have stroked for more than forty miles to get to the other shore. Perhaps the holder of the title for stick-to-itiveness is Jabez Wollfe. He tried to swim the channel twenty-one times and never made it.

Some other endurance and distance swimmers of note include John Sigmund, who swam 292 miles down the Mississippi River in eighty-nine hours, forty-two minutes. Daniel Carpio of Peru was the first to swim the Strait of Gibraltar from Spain to Morocco, a distance of eight miles. Tom Blower of England was first to swim the twenty-five miles across the Irish Sea from Northern Ireland to Scotland. And a woman, Myrtle Huddleston of New York, swam continuously in a pool for three days, fifteen hours, and twenty-seven minutes.

SURF BATHING

One form of swimming that thousands of people do just for the fun of it is called *surf bathing* or simply *surfing*. Just about everyone who can get to a sandy beach has tried surfing, provided the water's warm enough. But it wasn't always so. For many years, and in most countries, it was considered indecent to bathe in the surf in broad daylight. Laws were passed banning such a shocking display of the human form even when fully covered. (As late as 1935, male swimmers at New Jersey beaches were arrested if wearing topless swimsuits.)

You can thank a fellow named William Gocher, the crusading editor of a suburban newspaper near Sydney, Australia, for bringing surf bathing out into the sunlight. It happened in 1902. Gocher's newspaper office was in Manly, only a few yards from one of Australia's best-known beaches. He, like many another Aussie, besported himself in the surf before 1902. But he took his pleasure by moonlight because the law at the time stated that no person may publicly surf bathe on any beach between the hours of seven in the morning and seven at night. The usual thing was a refreshing dip in the briny after dark and another before the crack of dawn. As was appropriate for dunking in the dark, the most common "swimsuit" was a long nightshirt.

Town officials in many seaside towns, alarmed at such wickedness, arranged to have church bells rung an hour before dawn each day so the surfing members of the community could get themselves hence before the light of day revealed their shame.

Such goings-on distressed Editor Gocher. Since he enjoyed surf bathing, and possibly because his subscribers complained about the noise of early church bells, he decided to revolt. In a front-page editorial, he announced that he would enter the surf of Manly Beach at noon on the following Sunday to test the validity of the no-dipping-by-day law.

The citizens of Manly — in fact all Down Under — were staggered. Even those who crept to the shores by moonlight questioned the wisdom of choosing the Lord's day for the protest swim. Authorities added legal as well as moral arguments. But protests by churchmen and police only strengthened Gocher's resolve to carry out his plan.

Thus, when the churches let out on Sunday, the faithful and sinners alike hurried to the beach, where a crowd was gathering. When, at last, Gocher drove up in a carriage and stepped from it the startled mob grew hushed with what they saw. Instead of swimming attire, he was nattily dressed in a frock coat and striped trousers. Grey spats topped his polished shoes and a tall silk hat topped his neatly groomed head.

Some of the people present began to pray. Others struck up a hymn. Two police officers, their duty plain, stepped forward and warned Gocher that the moment his foot touched the water he would be under arrest.

The crusading editor ignored them and strode to the water's edge. The police followed on his heels and waited for the first wave to lap at his shoes. Suddenly Gocher leaped out of their reach and dashed into the surf, splashing and capering. The police stayed dry-shod on the beach.

Gocher was so obviously enjoying himself that the hymns died and cheers rose from the crowd. People laughed and applauded. When, at last, a billowing wave deposited the panting editor on the beach again, he was duly arrested and rushed off to a magistrate's office to be charged. The crowd followed, then carried him home in triumph on their shoulders to change into dry clothing.

Fanned by an all-out press campaign in his favor as well as the obvious support of public opinion, Gocher's campaign for daylight surfing was immediately successful. Charges against him were dismissed. The next weekend hundreds of men, women, and children — the first of millions — were enjoying the surf at Manly and a score of other beaches in the Sydney area. The law forbidding daylight surf bathing was ignored until it was formally repealed.

To date Hero, Leander swam four miles every night.

DIVING

Diving has been enjoyed ever since kids started going down to the creek for a dip. They do it off tree limbs, overhanging cliffs, railroad trestles, and anything else that hangs high or low over the water. Our name for the fun, *dive*, is another term that comes from Old English roots back when the scholars hadn't made up their minds on how to spell things. (Did you ever try to read one of Geoffrey Chaucer's *Canterbury Tales?*)

The word *dive* first appeared about the year 1300 and came from a mixture of words like *dufan*, meaning "to duck"; *dyfan*, meaning "to dip"; and *dyppan*, meaning both "dip" and "deep." Take your pick.

There's not much in ancient legend or even modern history about diving, unless you want to count Icarus, the Greek kid who made some artificial wings like his dad's and flew too close to the sun. The sun's heat melted the wax holding the wings together and Icarus took a dive.

Diving as a sport was first perfected and taught in Europe in the final portion of the nineteenth century. But it wasn't until 1904 at Paris that men's diving competitions were introduced in the Olympic Games. Women's diving was included at the Games in 1912. Various types of diving are now judged in the contests, such as *swan dive*, *back dive*, and *jack-knife*, but in the records they are listed in two main categories, *springboard* and *platform diving*.

Over the years since 1904, the United States has dominated the Olympic diving championships.

WATER POLO

Water polo, sometimes called a free-for-all while you soak your head, was first organized into a recognizable game in England in 1876 as a way of playing soccer in water. It's a team sport with eight players on a side. It gets its name from the polo played on horseback, but there are no ponies in the swim or any wooden mallets. And the ball used is inflated, not wooden. For this reason, you could say that *water polo* is misnamed, because the word *polo* comes from the Tibetan game on horseback called *pulu*. In its early days, water polo was called by several names — *aquatic football*, *aquatic handball*, and *water soccer*, for instance. Any one of them seems more on the mark than the present name. (See the section on polo in Chapter 25.)

Water polo has been an Olympic event since 1900. Since 1928, teams from Hungary have dominated the sport. In fact, one Hungarian, Dezso Gyarmati, won three Gold Medals plus a Silver and a Bronze in water polo, and was one of the few athletes in the world to win medals in five successive Olympics. Meanwhile, his family was busy collecting medals, too. Dezso's wife, Eva, won Gold and Silver Medals for the 200 meter breaststroke. Their daughter, Andrea, won Silver and Bronze Medals in backstroke and butterfly events.

SWIMMING QUIZ

Get in deeper. Explore the details of Lord Byron's swim across the Hellespont to test the legend of Leander's nightly swims to visit Hero. Answer this: How far did Lord Byron actually swim according to his own report?

Gocher brought surf bathing into the light of day.

4

Archery

A Sport of Gentlemen & Ladies

Archery is probably the oldest of our sports — though it wasn't a game for a very long time. Like several of today's pastimes, archery as a sport grew out of earlier skills developed for self-protection and survival. Bows and arrows were first used for hunting and defense.

No one knows when men first stretched bowstrings on *arcs* of bone or wood (the name is from the Latin word *arcus*, meaning "bow"). But it was surely more than thirty thousand years ago, because the remains of huge animals that were buried in the Ice Age have been found with stone arrowheads in their hides. Prehistoric rock paintings in Spain show men hunting with bows and arrows. And ancient pieces of bows made of wood, animal horns, and whalebone have been dug up, some of them with bits of gut and rawhide bowstrings still attached.

Many old tales, some true, some legend, mention the use of bows and arrows. For example, the Bible tells us that Jonathan, a friend of David, shot an arrow to where David was in hiding to give him warning of King Saul's continued anger. Even in those ancient days, Jonathan made it clear that targets were set up for archery practice. Referring to David's hiding place, he said, "I shall be shooting arrows toward it as though at a target."

Perhaps the best known legend in which a bow and arrow are involved is the one about Switzerland's national hero, William Tell. Tell was a leader in the Swiss War of Independence against the Austrians at the beginning of the fourteenth century. When he refused to "salute the cap" of the arrogant imperial governor named Gessler, Tell was sentenced to shoot an apple off the head of his son. He did it without turning a hair, but when he relaxed after the shot a second arrow fell from beneath his cloak. When the governor demanded to know what the extra arrow was for, Tell replied: "To shoot you with, had I failed in the task imposed upon me."

Gessler had Tell clapped in prison for that remark. But he was rescued by Swiss peasants, and later actually did shoot Gessler while helping free his country from Austrian rule.

There's only one thing wrong with this story. Nobody has ever had the courtesy to tell us the name of William Tell's son. It's okay for dad to be a hero, but the kid who was the target of the day and escaped by a hair's breadth ought to get more of the glory.

Archery buffs are "toxophiles," or "those fond of the bow."

Though the legend often says William Tell used a "bow and arrow," it is quite possible that he used a *crossbow* to remove the apple from his son's head. Crossbows were the most common weapon for hunting and war on the mainland of Europe at the time. But it is the *longbow*, developed in the British Isles, that we read most about in history books and novels. The longbow originated in Wales and even after it was adopted and popularized by the English, the bows tended to be the same height as the archers who carried them. The average then was five feet, six inches. The arrows were about half that length. (Halfway around the world, Japanese warriors were fighting with seven-foot bows.)

The English development and mastery of the longbow made it a potent weapon and changed the art of war. A good bowman could shoot six aimed shots per minute at a range of 200 yards. Greater distances were possible, but the practical limit was about 300 yards. This gave the English bowmen an advantage over foes with crossbows, which were slower to reload and shoot and had a shorter range. That's one reason why, from the thirteenth to the seventeenth century, there were laws in England requiring able-bodied men to engage in regular archery practice with the longbow. Other laws forbade such "frivolous" sports as football and golf because they took time away from archery practice.

Better weapons put an end to the enforced practice. Along came gunpowder and firearms, and the military longbow became about as useful as last year's exam questions. But even before the archers lost their jobs in the army they were forming recreational clubs to continue shooting as a sport. These amateurs adopted the Greek word *toxon*, meaning "bow," and called themselves *toxophiles*, "those fond of the bow." (Our modern word *toxic* also comes from *toxon* through association with the Greek term for arrow poison.)

As archery caught on as a sport, and even before longbows were discarded by the military, the first book on the subject was written in 1545 by a target shooter named Roger Ascham. It was a how-to handbook titled, *Toxophilus, the Schole of Shooting*, and, aiming for royal support, Ascham dedicated the book to King Henry VIII.

Organized archery societies began to flourish in the seventeenth century. But unlike many other sports, archery has always been an activity of *amateurs*, a term that the English first used to distinguish between the cultivated, aristocratic persons who had the time and money to engage in recreation and the commoners who entered sports for money. The word *professional* was first applied in 1512 to label hired jockeys who rode racehorses for a fee. The English spelling of *amateur* is a reworking of the Latin word *amator*, which means "lover." Thus an amateur is a person who does his or her thing for the love of it. For example, "Gentleman Jack" Jackson was an aristocrat who boxed just for fun, so British newspapers dubbed him an amateur to set him apart from the bare-knuckle fighters of the day who fought for small purses and side bets. The concept of an amateur as a cultivated person of leisure and a pro as a money-seeking ruffian persisted in England until the end of the nineteenth century.

Perhaps because of the genteel nature of archery, it has never been festooned with the load of wacky lingo and jargon found in some other sports. There's no hat trick (hockey), turkey (bowling), or Alibi Ike (baseball) here. On the other hand, the use of bows and arrows brought several interesting expressions into our everyday conversation. When a person makes a strong point in an argument, we say he or she *draws the longbow*. We say a person who is nervous or angry has become *unstrung*. Maybe you can think of others.

Of course, the Indians of North America have hunted with bows and arrows for uncounted centuries. Early settlers in Canada sometimes referred to the native tribes as the "bows and arrows." But archery did not emerge as an organized leisure sport on this side of the Atlantic until 1828, when a club, The United Bowmen of Philadelphia, was formed. What has happened since is evident in the fact that today there are more than ten million amateur archers in the United States alone.

In 1900 in Paris, the sport was included in the second meeting of the modern Olympic Games, and was repeated in 1904 and 1908. Women archers were first included in the Olympics in 1904 at St. Louis. An American woman listed in the records simply as Mrs. M.C. Howell won a Gold Medal in all three events. For various reasons, archery was dropped from the Games until 1920, then dropped again until 1972. However, it is one of two dozen "preferred" sports that must be considered for each Olympiad. Since the rules say at least fifteen of them must be included at each competition, chances are we'll continue to see archers at a good share of the Games.

The bow used at the Olympics in 1900-08 resembled the historic longbow. It hadn't changed in centuries, remaining plain and simple. But in recent years inventive archers have devised ways to alter and improve the tools of their sport. The target shooter and bow hunter of today can choose a variety of bows with personalized grips and aiming devices. There are even better *nocks* (notches) and *fletching* (feathers) for the arrows.

They've figured out new ways to compete, too, for accuracy and distance. One eager fellow built himself a *foot bow*, which he fired by sitting on the ground, pushing the bow with his feet, and drawing back on the string with both hands. (In archery this is called *free style shooting*.) Would you believe he shot an arrow a full mile with an extra 100 yards for good measure?

Pity nobody ever mentioned the name of William Tell's son.

ARCHERY QUIZ

Take a shot at these questions about championship archery:

1. What is the average length (in feet) of a bow in modern men's archery competition?
2. How long (in feet) are women's bows on average?
3. How long (in inches) are the arrows used in men's competition?
4. How long (in inches) are the women's arrows?
5. How much pull (in pounds) does the average man's bow require to draw the string back the length of the arrow?
6. How much pull (in pounds) does a women's bow need for the draw?
7. What is the diameter (in inches) of the inner circle (bull's-eye) of the target?
8. What is the official color of the bull's-eye?

5

Baseball

At the Start There was Much at Stake — Four of Them

HISTORY OF THE GAME

Want to catch your average baseball fan off base? Easy. Ask him or her who invented the modern game.

The odds are very good that the response will be "Abner Doubleday, everybody knows that." Then you say, "Gotcha! It wasn't Doubleday, it was Alexander Cartwright." That's right, Cartwright, a New York bank teller and part-time surveyor.

Most folks, however, still believe the legend that Doubleday invented the game in 1839 at Cooperstown, New York. This is unlikely, though, because Abner was a cadet at West Point at the time and probably was more concerned with making it in the army than getting to first base on a ball field. (Actually, he later rose to the rank of major-general in the Union army during the Civil War.)

On the other hand, there is documented proof that Cartwright formed a ball team called the Knickerbockers and on June 19, 1846 organized a game against a team called the New York Nine. The game was played at Hoboken, New Jersey. He may have regretted it, because the Knicks lost 23-1, but the significance of this first organized game in baseball history is that it was played according to rules devised by Cartwright and that these were the first written rules for the game. The rules still form the basis of the way baseball is played, and all rule changes since then can be traced back to this original list. For instance, Cartwright designed a baseball *diamond*

There is still some argument about who invented baseball.

with its corners ninety feet apart. Actually it's a square, but it's tilted onto a corner and looks like a diamond, so that's what they called it. Cartwright also established the nine playing positions, fixed the fair and foul territories, and ruled that each team would bat until it made three outs.

Baseball players will be forever grateful for something else Cartwright wrote into the rules. That's in the way putouts are made. Before the rules were written, a base runner was put out by throwing the ball at him. Cartwright introduced the tag rule, which is a lot less painful.

Despite all this, you'll still get arguments in favor of Abner Doubleday as "the father of modern baseball." A committee appointed by the U.S. Congress in 1907 to study the history of baseball said that Doubleday devised a scheme of play but never got around to writing down any rules. It's a good argument, providing you overlook the fact that the chairman of the committee, A.G. Mills, served with Doubleday in the army and maybe made a pitch for his friend. Anyway, the argument still goes on, but arguments are a feature of the game — on the diamond and off.

Those who disagree about who was the "father of modern baseball" also can't decide what was the granddaddy of the game itself. (With the possible exception of basketball, all of our modern sports can be traced back to something else.) Some say *cricket* was the forerunner of baseball, probably because of the bats. But there is more evidence that what is now the American national game developed from an English boys' game called *rounders*. A form of rounders was played in America even before the colonies became the United States. It usually was played on a square "diamond" marked by four stakes in the ground, and when the early catch-as-catch-can versions of baseball were devised, they were played on a staked-out square, too. The game was even called *Stake Ball*. Other names for the early games were *One Old Cat* and *Two Old Cat*.

Apparently the base runners and basemen got tired of tripping over the stakes, because slabs of stone were substituted to mark the corners of the diamond. Even these barked the shins of players sliding into them, so sand-filled sacks appeared, then the square, sand-filled canvas *bases* that are used today. Somewhere between the stone slabs and the arrival of canvas bags, the name *baseball* was adopted.

From the time the Knickerbockers and the New York Nine launched formal competition in 1845, the game of baseball spread slowly across the United States and Canada. Not everybody played by the same rules. Teams in Philadelphia played One Old Cat and in Boston they played a Beantown version of Rounders. Nevertheless, by 1860 there were more than ten clubs in New York, Brooklyn, and New Jersey playing baseball according to Alexander Cartwright's rules. The number of clubs continued to grow to the point that in 1857, sixteen New York and Brooklyn ball clubs met to form the National Association of Base Ball Players, the forerunner of baseball's *National League*.

The outbreak of the Civil War slowed the progress of baseball, but not the growing enthusiasm for the game. There were even instances during lulls in the conflict when temporary truces were declared and soldiers on both sides swapped guns for bats and played baseball until fighting resumed. After the war the game caught on rapidly. By 1868, when a convention of baseball clubs was held, delegates came from eighteen states and represented four hundred teams.

Team organizers soon learned to attract the best players by offering them money. The result: professional baseball with paid players and all-pro teams. In 1864, Alfred Reach, second baseman for the Philadelphia Athletics, became the first baseball player to receive pay for playing. The first fully professional season was in 1869. The undisputed stars were the Cincinnati Red Stockings, who set a win-loss record that has never been equalled. They ran up a score of sixty-five wins, no defeats, and a 17-17 tie with the Troy (New York) Haymakers. Appropriately, the name of the president of the club was Aaron B. Champion.

When Champion added up the club's season expenses for players' salaries and the cost of traveling 12,000 miles by boat, train, and stagecoach, the sum came to $29,724.87. (George Wright, the Cincinnati captain and shortstop, was paid $1,400. Compare that to the $100,000 minimum salary Big League players get today.) Balanced against the club's share of that first season's ticket sales, the Red Stockings made a total profit of $1.39! The second season they went in the hole financially. The team lost five games and the fickle fans deserted them in droves. To add to his woes, Champion was beset by what he called "enormous salary demands." So he disbanded the club. As you know, it was later reorganized, and the Cincinnati Reds are major contenders today.

Before the Red Stockings were disbanded, the team launched a new style of baseball uniform not unlike the kind modern players wear. Until 1867, the various teams wore uniforms of sorts, but they generally were white shirts and long trousers. Then a fellow named George Allard, who had played with the Cincinnati team as an amateur, had a bright idea. Allard obviously had some say in the team management because he ordered white flannel shirts, knee-length trousers, and bright red stockings for all players. The team got a new look and its name. Incidentally, the uniforms were made in the Cincinnati tailor shop of Mrs. Bertha Bertram—which makes her a sort of "Betsy Ross of baseball."

By 1875, it was obvious that professional baseball needed a governing organization to bring order to a chaotic jumble of minor leagues and associations. Nobody knew who the season's champions were because everybody had a claim on the title. The answer was the *National League*. It was formed that year, and the first league games were played in 1876. The eight charter members of the National League were teams in Boston, Chicago, Cincinnati, Hartford, Louisville, New York, Philadelphia, and St. Louis. A rival *American Association* was formed in 1882, planting the seed of what became the *American League* in 1901. From its beginning, the National organization was known as the *Big League*. The nickname was also given the American League, and both were called the *majors* by the press.

The first *World Series* of that name was played in 1884 between the Providence Nationals of the National League and the New York Metropolitans of what was to become the American League. Providence took the pennant, winning all three games.

Let's not overlook the amateurs. The first intercollegiate baseball game was played July 1, 1859, between Amherst and Williams College, both in Massachusetts. Everyone at bat must have belted out a hit or two, because Amherst won 66-32.

This was a time of much experimenting with new baseball equipment. For example, a catcher's glove, still unpadded, was introduced in 1875, and the first chest protectors for catchers appeared ten years later. A catcher's mask was invented in 1875 by Fred Thayer, who got the idea from the masks worn in fencing matches. The mask was first used in games played at Harvard, but it was some years before professional catchers would try it.

NICKNAMES AND LINGO

Over the years, sportswriters have written more about baseball than any other game. As a result, they've been responsible for many of the baseball terms, nicknames, and lingo we use today. Even the names of several major league teams are the products of sportswriters' fantasies or newspaper naming contests. For instance, the Kansas City *Royals* got their name in a newspaper's poll of fans. The Chicago *Cubs* and Cleveland *Indians* also were named in newspaper contests. Before the contests, the Chicago team had been called the *White Stockings*, *Colts*, and *Orphans*. The Cleveland players had been the *Spiders*, *Blues*, and *Molly McGuires*.

Back in the 1880s, somebody in the press box dubbed the fledgling Pittsburgh team the *Innocents* after they lost 113 of a string of 136 games. Later, when Pittsburgh lured a valuable second baseman away from the Philadelphia *Athletics*, a writer accused them of being *Pirates*. The name stuck.

Until 1901, the Boston team was known as the *Somersets* after the club owner. Then they became the *Puritans*, the *Plymouth Rocks*, and even the *Beaneaters*. When their rivals, the Boston *Nations*, discarded their red stockings in favor of white ones, the Beaneaters (or whatever) quickly donned red stockings and have been called the *Red Sox* ever since.

The Brooklyn (now Los Angeles) *Dodgers* once were called, of all things, the *Bridegrooms*. Then the press gave them their present name because the fans and players were *Trolley Dodgers* in the streets outside the Brooklyn ballpark. For more than a dozen years the team name was *Robins* after the club manager, Wilbert Robinson. Then it was back to Trolley Dodgers. Somewhere along the line, the Trolley was derailed in favor of the shorter name, Dodgers.

The *Cardinals* of St. Louis were named in 1889 when a sportswriter reported overhearing a woman fan saying she adored the cardinal red trim on the players' uniforms. The New York *Yankees* were originally called the *Highlanders*, but nobody knows why. And, though there once was a Philadelphia team named the *White Elephants*, the *Phillies* have always had that name. Likewise the Baltimore *Orioles*. They took the name of a former team in Baltimore before the turn of the century. The Cincinnati *Reds*, nee Red Stockings, is the oldest team name in major league baseball.

Some baseball jargon and expressions are now everyday language and vice versa. For example, "Slide, Kelly, slide!" There actually was a *Kelly* in baseball, just as there was an *Annie Oakley* and a *Charley Horse*. But there never was a real *Casey* at the bat.

The famous slider was Michael Joseph Kelly, a catcher and outfielder in the 1880s for teams in Cincinnati, Chicago, New York, and Boston. He was a great base runner and when he tried to steal a base the fans would yell, "*Slide, Kelly, slide!*" Newspapers picked up the phrase and implanted it in our language.

We often hear a base on balls referred to as an *Annie Oakley*. It's another way of saying a "free pass" or "free ticket." In the last century, it was the custom to mark free tickets to events by punching a hole in them. Thus, the freebies came to be known as "Annie Oakleys" with a nod to the famous female crack shot who was noted for shooting holes in playing cards. The term was picked up in baseball when referring to a free trip to first base.

You'll get an argument about the origin of the term *Charley Horse*, which is used when ball players — and fans, too — get a painful cramp in the leg. One theory is that the term should be spelled "charley horse" without capital letters because it comes from Charley "Duke" Esper, a major league pitcher in the 1890s who had a gimpy gait like a lame horse. Others say we get the term from Charley, a horse used by groundskeepers to pull a heavy roller around the infield of the Chicago White Sox ballpark. Charley had a peculiar limp, and anybody who walks like him surely has a charley horse.

About *Casey*, mentioned earlier. He wasn't a real person, but next to Babe Ruth, he's probably the world's best-known ball player. Casey is the subject of Ernest Thayer's famous poem, "Casey at the Bat," which has been read and recited by millions of people. The poem tells of a tense ninth inning in which Casey comes to bat with two out and two runners on base. His team is trailing, but a home run by Casey will turn the tide. You know the ending. The mighty Casey struck out and "there is no joy in Mudville tonight." The poet surely wasn't a sportswriter. He tells us of the batting order ahead of Casey — Cooney, Barrows, Flynn, and Jimmy Blake. But he never mentions the name of the hero of the game, the pitcher who whiffed the mighty Casey.

Another famous, but fictional, baseball player we often refer to is *Alibi Ike*. He's a character originated by Ring Lardner in a 1915 short story and he has even been portrayed in a movie. Alibi Ike is a player who has an excuse for every error or strikeout he makes. He's also known as a *Club House Lawyer*, and, if you play baseball or any other team sport, you've already met the guy.

In case you're wondering, the word *umpire* is a modern spelling of a Middle English word, *noumper*, which meant a person brought in to settle an argument between two others. Alexander Cartwright used the term "umpire" when he wrote the first baseball rules in 1845. He got it from rounders, or possibly cricket.

Baseball historians seem to agree that *bunt* is an early misspelling of the word *butt*, which more or less describes how the batter is trying to use the bat to hit the ball. But nobody can agree on one of the several theories of how *bullpen* got into baseball lingo. A prominent guess is that bullpen comes from the prison term for a large caged area. The separate area reserved for warming up pitchers was thought to be similar. That's a lot of bull, say some historians — the term really comes from early days when pitchers warmed up at the far outer edge of fair territory. There often was a huge Bull Durham Tobacco sign there and the pitchers warmed up where the big painted bull was — in the bullpen.

As you might have guessed, a *pinch hitter* is a batter called on "in a pinch." But did you know that *grand slam*, meaning a home run hit when the bases are loaded, is a term borrowed from a card game, contract bridge? Baseball writers adopted it first, but it's now also heard in golf and tennis circles.

By now you are ready for a *seventh inning stretch*. That's baseball jargon for the pause after the top half of the seventh inning when everybody stands up and stretches. There are a number of stories about how the custom started, but the most accepted one comes from a season-opening game in Washington in 1910. President William Howard Taft was there to toss out the first ball and he stayed to watch the game. When he rose to stretch his legs in the middle of the seventh inning, the fans thought he was leaving, so everybody stood up out of respect for the Presidency.

There's much more. In fact, baseball is so loaded with strange tales and language that a sportswriter named Patrick Ercolano compiled a whole dictionary on the sport. Its title is *Fungoes, Floaters and Fork Balls*, which gives you some idea what anybody wanting to talk baseball is up against. It's a whole new lingo.

BASEBALL QUIZ

Here are some double plays to take a swing at. Some baseball terms have two or more meanings. They've been borrowed for the game from other sources or have gone into everyday language from baseball. "Double header" is an example. It's a railroad term for a train with two engines. It was railroad lingo long before it was used in baseball. Here are several more terms doing double duty. Write the baseball meaning for each, plus a second meaning:

Big League	Dugout
Bush League	Fireball
Charley Horse	Goose Egg
Diamond	Hardball

Also take a crack at: on deck, pinch hit, rain check, swat, and windup.

6

Basketball
A Peachy Game in a Cage

There's no need to prowl back through ancient Greek, Latin, or any other languages to find the source of the name *basketball*. Compared with most sports, basketball is a new kid on the block, only just over 100 years old. And it gets its name from the one-bushel peach baskets that were the first goals used in the game.

Now North America's leading indoor school sport, basketball was dreamed up by a Canadian-born Presbyterian minister, Dr. James A. Naismith. In the winter of 1891, while teaching at the International YMCA Training School in Springfield, Massachusetts, he devised a new indoor game in the hope of attracting more youths off the streets and into the "Y". (See Chapter 23 on volleyball for another sport launched at the Springfield school.)

Dr. Naismith reasoned that team games were usually played with some kind of ball. So he built the game rules around a handy soccer ball that hadn't been used since the cold weather drove most games indoors. But any similarity to soccer or football ended there. The good parson wanted to keep the roughness of physical contact out of the game as much as possible so that more boys could and would take part. Thus, in the thirteen rules he wrote in December 1891, it was forbidden to touch the ball with anything but the hands. Deliberate body contact (fouling) was banned.

A goal. What to use for a goal? Dr. Naismith wanted goals to be scored more through skill than by speed or muscle (he never dreamed there would be a slam dunk). Again he turned to something handy and available at the school — two empty peach baskets. These he fastened to the balconies at the ends of the gymnasium ... and fastened the name *basket ball* to the game at the same time. The single word, *basketball*, did not become official until 1921.

The new game, sometimes called *peach ball* because of the original use for the baskets, took off like a jump shot. It spread rapidly across the United States and Canada in YMCA's, high schools, colleges, and sports clubs. When girl teams took up the sport, they sometimes proved to be more fiercely competitive and serious about training than the boys.

The enthusiasm for basketball was so keen that in 1895, less than four years after the first ball landed in a peach basket, the first intercollegiate basketball game was held. It pitted a team from the Minnesota State School of Agriculture against Hamline College in St. Paul. Professional teams also made their appearance right from the start, playing in vacant store buildings, warehouses, and gymnasiums wherever space could be found.

One year Cornell played with fifty players on each side.

Within four years of its introduction in Springfield, the game was taken by YMCA graduates to China, Mexico, India, and France. By the turn of the century, Japanese and Persian (now Iranian) players were enthusiastically dribbling, passing, and sinking lay-ups in baskets of their own. With the end of World War I, the first international basketball tournament was held in Paris in 1919 as part of the Inter-Allied Games, which matched athletes and teams from the several allied military forces. Dr. Naismith was on hand with General John Pershing, commander-in-chief of the American forces, to watch the final basketball game and present the championship trophy. It went to the United States team. They clobbered a French team by a score of 93-8.

As the game gained in popularity, the rules and equipment changed with it. A regulation basketball, slightly larger than the original soccer ball, was adopted. The peach baskets were quickly replaced by cylindrical wire baskets, making it unnecessary to put up a ladder and fish out the ball every time a goal was scored. The wire baskets had chain pulls that opened the bottom and let the ball drop out. By 1893, the metal hoop with cord netting that we know today, as well as the backboard, had been introduced. The backboard not only prevented the ball from going astray in the gymnasium balconies, it prevented over-eager fans from using their hands and umbrellas to boost their team's shots into the hoop or to block the shots of visitors.

At the beginning, basketball had nine players on each side. But the number was a matter of local choice. Cornell University played one year with fifty men on each side! The spectators complained that they often lost sight of the ball in the milling crowd. So did many of the players. In 1896, the University of Chicago met the University of Iowa in Iowa City in the first college game with five players on each team. Word got around and within a year nearly all the colleges with basketball teams followed suit. Meanwhile, girl cagers usually chose to play with six players on each side. But in recent years, more and more of them have switched to five-player teams, especially in major tournaments.

It's easy to see why the players of this popular sport are called *basketeers* and *hoopsters*. But what about the nickname *cagers*? If you guess that the name comes from the high wire fences around outdoor basketball courts, you're off the mark ... but not far. When the first National Basketball League of six professional teams was formed in 1898, they enclosed their indoor courts with heavy wire mesh eleven feet high. The purpose was less to keep the ball in the court than to keep unruly spectators out of it. Watching the teams enclosed like monkeys in a circus cage, sportswriters were quick to dub the players "cagers." The wire mesh was ruled out in 1929 because too many players were getting scratched and scraped on the wire, but the nickname is still widely used.

Many basketball buffs get very excited at a game, while other spectators claim it's from dullsville. The great sportswriter Red Barber was among the latter. Once when asked what he thought of basketball, Barber said he could get more excitement watching paint dry. That was probably before the twenty-four-second clock appeared. Back then a team that didn't want their opponents to get their hands on the ball could pass and dribble it among themselves as long as they pleased without shooting for a goal. The game could drag on and on with little or no change in score.

For example, when the Minneapolis Lakers faced the Fort Wayne Pistons on November 22, 1950, the Lakers went into a slow-motion dribble and pass act to prevent the Pistons from getting the ball. Amid boos from the bored spectators, the first half ended with a score of only 13-11 in favor of the Lakers. There was more sleep-walking in the second period until, with nine seconds to go, the Pistons edged ahead to win the game 19-18. Shortly afterward a rule was inserted in pro basketball that requires a team to shoot for a goal within twenty-four seconds of getting possession of the ball. The result is a faster, more exciting game.

An interesting sidelight of basketball has been the feats of endurance and marathon games staged from time to time, usually to raise funds for good causes and for school equipment. For example, in 1965, a team of thirty students at Luther College in Wisconsin dribbled a basketball non-stop for thirty miles. Then in 1971, a popular year for marathon basketball, two teams at Brockville Collegiate Institute in Ontario raised money for scholarships by playing for 120 hours. They chalked up a score of 10,102 to 9,256. Not to be outdone, students at Whitewater State University in Wisconsin helped pay for a new swimming pool by playing basketball for 240 consecutive hours and a final score of 25,540 to 25,510.

Here's a late score on the invention of basketball. Though Dr. Naismith is given well-deserved credit for launching today's game near the end of the nineteenth century, archaeologists have since discovered a game similar to basketball played by the Aztecs in the

Andes Mountains of South America. Their ancient game was played on a court walled with stones. A large stone ring was set vertically in the wall at each end of the court. The ball was tossed through the stone ring to score.

The Aztecs must have taken their sport very seriously. The captain of the losing team was usually beheaded. It has been suggested that this was to teach him to try harder the next time.

Basketball was invented to get young men inside and off the streets.

BASKETBALL QUIZ

As basketball rolled across the country faster than Hula-Hoops™ many schools and athletic clubs didn't wait for a set of Dr. Naismith's rules. As a result, there was much confusion when teams with different rules met to play. Some of this early confusion is reflected in present day regulations. For example:

1. Can you give the length and width of a regulation basketball court?

2. The present regulation ball is about thirty inches around. What is its weight?

3. Basketball players play three positions, which were adopted from football and hockey. Do you know what they are called?

4. What are the two principal differences between amateur and professional basketball?

7

Bowling

A Game the Gamblers almost Ruined

PIN BOWLING

Early in this century, excavators digging in the ancient tomb of an Egyptian child unearthed a ball and nine stone "pins" among other toys. Since the child had died in 5200 B.C., this would seem to tell us that our game of *bowling* is a very old game indeed. It would also seem to knock the pins out from under a general belief that bowling was invented by German monks sometime in the third or fourth century.

Maybe, just maybe, both ideas could be true. Bowling as we know it could have been a very ancient game, so old that it had time to die out, then be re-invented again. We don't see any mention of bowling at pins in Greek and Roman legends, but we have lots of documented tales about how the practice of rolling a ball at a set of pins was the brainstorm of German monks. Maybe they came up with the game on their own at the time and in the way most people like to think. After all, the monks made a religious ceremony of bowling. It wasn't until later that they realized they could bowl just for fun.

What happened was that the monks made use of an object that just about every German male carried with him. That was his *kegel*, a short, knobbly staff something like our "modern" Indian club. No self-respecting fellow would be caught without one, because his kegel had so many uses. It could be twirled and whirled to

German clerics rolled a ball at a kegel to "strike down the devil."

strengthen his wrists and arms. It could be used in fights, in crude fencing matches, and in friendly throwing contests. A kegel was also handy for hammering nails and smashing cockroaches.

The monks, on the other hand, saw in the ever-present kegel a way of testing the faith of ordinary citizens. The cloisters of their churches usually had long, narrow, covered galleries with about the same dimensions as a present-day bowling alley. A man suspected of straying from the path of righteousness would be called to the cloister, and his kegel would be set on its end far along one of these galleries. Then he would be given a round stone and told to roll it along the gallery at his kegel.

Sounds like great fun, doesn't it? But the brothers were deadly serious. This was a religious rite to them. The kegel represented "Heide," the heathen — or devil. If the man being put to the test knocked down his kegel with the stone, it proved he was leading a Christian life. If he missed, aha!, he was labelled a sinner and told to mend his ways. In addition, he had to come back every now and then to bowl at his kegel until he got a strike and, praise the Lord, was no longer judged a sinner.

The trouble with this ritual was that even the worst sinner in town could get off scot-free if he was a good *kegler* (that's where sportswriters got their term for *bowler*). So the practice was abandoned as a religious rite at some time in the fifth century. Meanwhile the monks, who also carried kegels, had been amusing themselves by doing just what they had required suspected sinners to do. They even took their game a bit further by arranging several kegels in a group and taking turns rolling the stone ball at them. The brother who knocked down the most kegels won what was obviously the great granddaddy of our modern bowling contests. They liked the game so much that they soon took it outside the cloisters and let ordinary laymen in on the fun.

Some say the game's present name, *bowling*, comes from an old German word *bolon*, meaning "to roll." But since the game soon spread to other countries in Europe, it is possible we got the name of the game from *boule*, the French word for "ball," or *bowle* as the English first spelled it.

In any event, the game became very popular throughout most of Europe. In the Middle Ages, castles and large estates all had bowling alleys in their courtyards and gardens. Army barracks and state schools had them, too, especially in Germany. Town celebrations and even church festivals included bowling matches among the special events. Nor was it entirely a male sport. A painting done in Switzerland in 1530 shows a woman about to heave a ball down a bowling alley in a garden while a male companion looks on.

But what was bowling in one town wasn't necessarily so down the turnpike. The game had no set rules for a long time and any number of pins were used. The Germans usually bowled at three pins until the fourteenth century. Elsewhere in Europe, as many as seventeen pins were used. When bowling indoors, the ball was rolled at the pins. But when bowling out-of-doors, the ball could be rolled or thrown at them, take your pick. It was not until sometime in the 1500s that rules for a nine-pin game were standardized by none other than Martin Luther, the noted religious reformer. Luther took the time from church duties to be an avid and expert kegler.

With nine pins needed, the players began carving them from wood specifically for use in the game. They also made pins of bone, usually the shank bones of farm animals. Wooden balls succeeded the original stone ones, and the balls began to get larger. When they became so big it was hard to get a handle on them, somebody had a bright idea and drilled finger holes in the balls. Even in the earliest times, indoor bowling alleys were surfaced with wood. But the ones outside were made of beds of hard clay or tamped-down cinders.

Once their game was moved out of the cloisters and from under the watchful eyes of the monks, pin bowlers made a big thing of betting on the results. The sport was taken over by gamblers, both amateur and professional. This may be a reason why at first pin bowling wasn't accepted with much enthusiasm in England, Scotland, and Ireland. In fact, such large sums were being won and lost in England in 1332 that King Edward IV issued a law forbidding "casting a bowle at ninepins of wood or nine shank-bones of an ox or a horse." It was a long, long time before bowling at pins got any respect in the British Isles.

The exact date that bowling crossed the ocean to North America is obscured because written references to "bowling" often do not make it clear whether the writer was referring to the nine-pin variety or lawn bowling (explained later in this chapter). It is generally conceded that lawn bowling was introduced into what is now New York by the Dutch in about 1690. The original bowling green in New York City has long since been paved over, but the area around Battery Park is still called Bowling Green. Bowling at pins may not have come over from Europe any sooner than 1800. The first definite reference to this game was made in 1819 when Washington Irving wrote the tale of Rip Van Winkle in his *Sketch Book*. He wrote of the thunder of balls striking pins and was so casual about the reference that one gets the impression bowling at pins had been around for some time.

From New York, nine-pin bowling found its way throughout New England and as far south as Washington, DC. But, alas, the gamblers took over the game just as they had done earlier in Europe. Huge bets were made and there were near-riots when it was suspected that some of the matches were "fixed." Goons hanging around the bowling alleys often beat up the bowlers who caused them to lose bets. The situation became so bad in New Haven and Hartford that the Connecticut legislature passed a law banning the game of "bowling at 9 pins."

That Connecticut statute is the reason we have ten-pin bowling today. It specifically prohibited nine-pin bowling, so somebody devised a game using ten pins to get around the law. Despite its sneaky origin, the new game was happily accepted by honest bowlers, too. But when the bowling lanes again became infested with gamblers, hoodlums, and hustlers, honest bowlers who preferred the game simply for recreation banded together to form an organization that could keep out the shady element. The result was the *American Bowling Congress*, formed September 9, 1895 in New York City.

The first task of the ABC was to standardize the ten-pin game. New rules were written and the dimensions of alleys and equipment were prescribed. Eventually, in 1901, the first national championship tournament was held in Chicago. There were 464 bowlers present and prizes for the winners amounted to $1,592. But the gamblers weren't invited. By 1916, so many women were bowling that the Women's International Bowling Congress was formed, and the first women's championship tournament was held the following year. Today, no one knows how many bowlers there are because only a small portion of the total are registered with the ABC and WIBC. But educated guesses put the total at up to thirty million male and female bowlers in the United States alone.

Every popular sport has some different forms, and avid bowlers have come up with new forms of their sport, too. *Duck Pins*, for example. It's a game for people who don't like to lift and roll the big, heavy balls used in the ten-pin game. Duck pins are so named because they are short and squat and "look like sitting ducks." In one form of the game, the pins have rubber "bumpers" around their waists. The balls are small enough to fit in the palm of your hand. Another game is *candle pins*. The small ball is used here, too, but the wooden pins are tall and slender like candles that bulge a bit in the middle.

LAWN BOWLING

Speaking of bowling with small balls, let's take a look at an entirely different form of the sport. Even as bowling at pins was catching on across Europe, a much older game was already being played. This was *lawn bowls*, later called *lawn bowling*. As the name indicates, it was played on a lawn of closely-cropped grass, and it also differed from the other bowling game because there were no pins to knock down. The first bowler rolled a small white ball across the grass, then he and each succeeding bowler tried to roll their balls closest to it or knock an opponent's ball away from it. This principle is a variation on the Italian game of *boccie* and was later copied in the sport of curling on ice, but more about that in another chapter.

The roots of the modern game of lawn bowling are older than those of bowling at pins. Traces of it have been found in Egypt, Greece, and Rome dating back more than 4,000 years, and we know that during the reigns of the Roman Caesars they definitely were playing the lawn bowls game. They called their game *boccie*, and the Italians still hold to that name.

The Roman legionnaires are believed to have taken the game with them when they invaded Britain in the year 43 A.D. Of course, the Britons, who seldom left an imported word alone, changed the name for boccie to *bowles*. They later changed that, too, calling the game *lawn bowls* so it wouldn't be confused with the bowling at pins. They liked both games, but the gentry took to lawn bowls, probably for two reasons. One, the pin game was considered a low class sport infested by gamblers, and two, the gentry had estates with ample lawn space for bowling greens (plus servants to cut the grass). They also were copying the royalty of mainland Europe where most of the castles and large estates had their own bowling greens. *Greens* in this case meant any flat grassy plot large enough to accommodate an *alley* 120 feet long and 20 feet wide. Many greens had more than one alley so that several games could be played at the same time. Both men and women could play and, since lawn bowling is not a strenuous game, the players tended to be the senior citizens of the day. This is a characteristic of the sport that still holds true.

Soon, however, all was not innocent fun for the old folks on the bowling greens. High-stakes betting began again and gamblers crashed the gates. By 1511, things were so far out of hand that King Henry VIII issued an edict declaring that "bowling has ceased to be a sport, and rather is a form of vicious gambling." His disapproval was principally aimed at bowling at pins, which he said "is an evil because the alleys are operated in conjunction with saloons or dissolute places." But the king included lawn bowling in the ban as well.

This ban on bowling in England actually remained in the law books until 1845, but nobody paid much attention to it. As a matter of fact, most of the English monarchs who followed Henry VIII were fair bowlers themselves and had bowling greens of their own.

As was mentioned earlier, the Dutch brought lawn bowling to New York at the end of the seventeenth century. Their original bowling green at the tip of Manhattan Island has long since been paved over, but the area around Battery Park at the lower end of Broadway is still known as Bowling Green. The game became the leading leisure-time sport in New York and Boston. Apparently there were commercial bowling greens operating much on the order of today's bowling lanes, because a 1714 advertisement in the "Boston News Letter" announced:

> "The Bowling Green, formerly belonging to Mr. James Ivers, Cambridge Street, now belongs to Daniel Stevens, of the British Coffee House, where all gentlemen, merchants, and others, having a mind to recreate themselves, shall be accommodated."

Of course, lawn bowling spread to other cities along the East Coast and into Canada, but it stopped short when the Revolutionary War broke out, being branded "an English game." After the war, nobody seemed much interested in resuming the game and it faded out in the fledgling United States for an entire century. The game's revival in this country can be credited to Christian Schepflin, who lived in Dunellen, New Jersey. Schepflin spent some time in England and Scotland and while there got hooked on lawn bowling. When he returned home, he laid out a green and explained the game to friends and neighbors. Thus, the sport's revival was on its way.

Lawn bowling has never made it to the Olympic Games, and neither has bowling at pins, but today lawn bowling is enjoyed by men and women around the world, particularly in English-speaking countries (with a nod to the boccie players in Italy). There are tens of thousands of players in nearly every country where the sport is found. Lawn bowling is especially popular Down Under. The first World Lawn Bowls Championship matches were held in Sydney, Australia in 1966. Bowlers from sixteen countries were on hand, including teams from the South Sea islands of Fiji and Papua-New Guinea.

Signs of bowling have been found in ancient Egyptian tombs.

BOWLING QUIZ

These questions ought to be right down your alley. Several actions and situations in modern bowling have geographical locations as nicknames. Can you explain the meaning in bowling of each of the following?

1. A Brooklyn

2. Dutch 200

3. Jersey Hit

4. New York Hit

5. Turkey

6. Worcester

8

Boxing
A Sport that Makes Fighters Toe the Mark

For centuries, the art of boxing was known as *pugilism*, which is rooted in the Latin word *pugnus*, meaning "one who fights with his fists." A pugnacious person you might say, and a reason why sportswriters call pugilists by the shorter name, *pug*.

Pugilism and pugilist are still used, of course, mainly by people who go in for high-toned words. But you're not a low-brow if you use the much newer word *boxing*. That one may be traced back to the Greek *puxos* and *pyx*, both of which mean either a "clenched fist" or anything "in the shape of a box." That's why we say a kid will "get his ears boxed" if he gets out of line.

You may find *fisticuffs* on the sports pages, too. That word came into being when two Middle English words were combined, but it's now used mostly as slang.

No matter what you call it, boxing as a sport is so old that nobody knows when or how it got started. We know that Egyptian warriors sometimes fought hand-to-hand with methods resembling boxing. Hieroglyphics inside the pyramids tell of it. A stone slab found in Iraq and dated about 4,000 years ago clearly shows two fighters in a boxing stance and with their fists wrapped in strips of leather. If those ancient boxers had wised up enough to wrap their fists in leather, it can be assumed that some prehistoric types were punching each other out long before that.

The sport next cropped up in Crete and then in Greece, where a legendary boxing and wrestling champ was a pug named Milton. He made a name for himself by carrying a full-grown bull around the Olympia stadium on his shoulders. Then he killed the bull with one blow of his fist and — would you believe? — ate it.

Despite the earlier sports news from Egypt and Iraq, historians generally give the credit for "organized" boxing to Theseus, a Greek sportsman who lived about 900 B.C. He was a good athlete himself and always ready for a fight. And since his father was king of Athens, he could organize bouts between Greek soldiers when

Early boxers punched until their opponents were dead.

they weren't out battling enemies. The trouble with Theseus, however, was a bloodthirsty streak in his nature. He wasn't satisfied with boxing matches like we have today. The opponents in his boxing matches literally fought to the finish, that is until one or the other was stone cold dead. The two fighters sat face-to-face on flat stones and slugged it out. Talk about hitting a man when he's down! When one boxer knocked the other unconscious, he kept on punching until the life was beaten out of the downed man. The fans got their money's worth, but Theseus was harder to please.

At first, the boxers in his matches wrapped their fists in strips of leather. But Theseus, a real Mr. Nasty, figured that slowed down the action, because some boxers could take a lot of punishment and refused to fall over. So Theseus put flat pieces of metal in the leather wrappings. Then, still dissatisfied, he replaced the metal discs with sharp metal spikes. With boxing "gloves" like that, it didn't take long for one or both of the opponents to go down for the final count.

Fighting with those rules, it's surprising anybody got to be champion for very long. But there was a bruiser named Theogenes from Thasos, Greece who has never been topped. If the ancient records can be believed, he is still the world's all-time boxing champion. Theogenes was so powerful and quick he usually got in the first punch and didn't need much more. In all, he beat 1,425 opponents to death! Another account says he knocked out more than 2,100 challengers, killing 1,800 of them.

When the Romans conquered Greece, they added an international flavor to boxing by introducing Roman versus Greek matches. Unfortunately, the use of metal spikes and other brutal devices in the fist coverings was continued, and still heavier weights were added to make the boxers' blows more effective. The leather binding with its metal attachments was called a *cestus*.

The Romans also introduced two features into boxing that brought it closer to what the sport is today. First, they got the boxers up off their stone seats to fight on their feet. Having done that, they marked off a limited area in which the fighters could slug it out. It is possible that the marked area was a circle, thus explaining how the word *ring* came to be applied to the roped-off square now used in boxing.

Like the Greeks, the Romans made a big thing of boxing. They honored and rewarded their champions and staged the best matches every holiday and even as a part of burial services for bigwigs. But eventually it dawned on the emperor (nobody seems to know which one) that bashing the brains out of his best warriors every holiday just didn't make sense. This gentleman banned the use of the brutal cestus and thus launched the sport of bare-knuckle fighting at the Forum. But not for long. Just at the beginning of the Christian era, another Roman emperor decided fighting with the fists wasn't proper training for military service, so he banned boxing altogether.

The history of boxing drew a blank for the next seventeen centuries — except for one isolated instance. The exception was in Siena, Italy, in about 1200 A.D., where hot-tempered men were in a habit of settling disputes with knives. A gentle priest taught them to use the "art of self defense" with fists instead. Partly because of this peaceable work, the priest was later canonized as St. Bernardine.

Alas, at the death of St. Bernardine, the heyday of boxing in Siena came to an end. What's more, the sport is unrecorded in all Europe until it surfaced once more in the seventeenth century in England. Considering the worldwide status of the sport today, don't be surprised to see historians referring to England as "the cradle of pugilism."

The style of bare-knuckle boxing at this time is best described as freewheeling. In addition to pummeling an opponent with his fists, a boxer could also lift him and hurl him to the ground. If done with force enough to knock the wind out of the opponent, he couldn't get up and the hurler won the bout. It wasn't exactly a gentlemen's game, but it wasn't a fight to the death either. Oddly, though there had been a supposed seventeen-century-long interval in European boxing, this rough-and-tumble way of fighting is similar to an ancient Greek sport called *pancratium*, a combination of boxing and wrestling. There were two types of pancratium. One was fought on hands and knees, the other while standing.

The man said to be most responsible for putting an end to the boxing-wrestling style in England, and then the world, was James Figg, an all-round good athlete. He liked the bare-knuckle boxing and soon learned that a hard punch to the jaw was faster and did more damage than a wrestling hold. So when an opponent stretched out his arms in an attempt to grapple with him, Figg slipped in a fast left or right hook. The result was a knockout or at least a punch that turned the other fellow to jelly so more blows could easily be landed.

By 1719, when Figg was only twenty-three years old, he had

run up an unbroken string of fifteen victories and had opened Figg's Academy of Boxing. Several of his students later opened boxing schools of their own, spreading the popularity of stand-up, bare-knuckle fighting with no wrestling involved.

If there was a flaw in this, it was Figg's idea of how a fight should proceed. His bouts had no *rounds* with rest periods in between. The two boxers simply started battling each other and threw punches until one was clearly the winner. It wasn't until 1743 that a fellow named Jack Broughton brought the idea of "rounds" to boxing. He wrote seven rules for a single match he was to referee, and one of these rules stated that when a fighter went down, a round was ended and his seconds had thirty seconds to get him back on his feet and ready to fight again. Another rule said, "... no person is to hit his adversary when he is down, or seize him by the hair, the breeches, or any part below the waist; a man on his knees is reckoned down."

Incidentally, Rule Number 1 gave birth to an expression we often use when talking of other things. It described a small square marked in chalk at the center of the ring. At the start of a round a fighter had to *toe the mark* and was considered beaten if he failed to do so.

The Broughton way of fighting took some of the brutality out of boxing and soon was being copied in all matches. With some revisions, including the title *London Prize Ring Rules*, these rules governed boxing for more than 100 years. But there was a flaw in the Broughton rules, too. They said a round was ended when a fighter went down on his knees. If a fighter was getting the worst of it, this rule gave him an out. When he was in trouble or simply tired, he could simply drop to his knees to end the round and then take a half-minute rest in his corner. At the end of the rest period, if he still didn't feel up to taking more punches, all he had to do was stagger to the mark in the middle of the ring and drop to his knees again without being hit. That ended another round, and he could take another thirty-second rest. Of course, his opponent was getting the rest periods, too, so a bout could go on and on with few punches thrown.

The most famous incident of this sort happened in the United States during a bare-knuckle championship battle between John L. Sullivan and Jake Kilrain. The fight was staged in Richburg, Mississippi, on July 8, 1889. Kilrain took advantage of the down-ends-the-round rule so often that the "fight" lasted two hours, sixteen minutes, and twenty-three seconds. Finally, he was unable to totter out and toe the mark in the seventy-fifth round. In that same year, two fighters named Dal Hawkins and Freddie Bogan battled for seventy-five rounds in San Francisco. The fight was interrupted because of darkness, and when they met again the next morning, Hawkins KOed Bogan in the fifteenth round. But they didn't break the record for the longest bare-knuckle fight in history. It happened in 1856 in Melbourne, Australia, when Jim Kelly and Jack Smith slugged it out for 186 rounds, lasting six hours and fifteen minutes.

Sullivan lost his world championship title to Jim Corbett three years later in New Orleans. Both fighters wore gloves and fought under the new *Marquis of Queensberry Rules*, a set of regulations that established a blueprint for modern boxing matches. The Marquis, aided by a man named John G. Chambers, wrote the rules in 1865, but they weren't all used in boxing matches until 1872. The most significant features the Queensberry Rules brought to boxing are the wearing of padded gloves, three-minute rounds, and a ban on wrestling (holding), throwing, and eye gouging.

Bare-knuckle fighting was very slow catching on in the United States and Canada, partly because several major cities declared the sport "barbarous" and "bestial" and banned it from their city limits. For a time there seemed as many battles in courtrooms and legislatures as there were in the ring. But with the arrival of the Queensberry Rules, boxing became more respectable and was at first tolerated, then grew in popularity. Even John L. Sullivan, the bare-knuckle champ, saw the writing on the locker room wall and helped popularize boxing with gloves.

Meanwhile, the organization and even the legality of boxing were slightly punch-drunk. Some of the "champions" were self-proclaimed and often ignored. Every state had its own rules for boxing or banned it entirely. Not until 1920 did the New York state legislature legalize the sport, an act that triggered similar laws in other states. Eventually the various state boxing commissioners banded together to form the *National Boxing Association*, the present ruling body for professional boxing in this country.

Boxing was included in the ancient Olympic Games as early as 688 B.C. An Armenian athlete named Varazdetes was the last bare-knuckle champion when the games were abolished in 393 A.D. He was so esteemed by his fellow countrymen that they elected him king of Armenia. When Olympic competition was revived at

Athens in 1896, boxing was considered, but was not included in the Games until 1904 at St. Louis. The United States boxing team won Gold Medals in all seven weight divisions.

There are many interesting, exciting, and just plain wacky tales about boxing. Among them is the case of two English women, perhaps the first to make a try at the sport. They developed a dislike for each other and as a result in June, 1722 the following notice appeared in a London newspaper:

> "Challenge — I, Elizabeth Wilkinson, of Clerkenwell, having had some words with Hannah Hyfield, and requiring satisfaction, do invite her to meet me upon the stage and to box for three guineas; each woman holding half a crown in each hand, and the first woman that drops the money to lose the battle."

Not to worry, neither Elizabeth nor Hannah dropped a coin or lost her guineas. To the great disappointment of a gathering audience, the police got there first. They claimed the fight would "violate decency" and if the ladies laid a hand on one another they would be tossed in the pokey.

In boxing's professional ranks, one champion in particular should be remembered, not for any offbeat reason but because he never lost a professional fight. He is Rocky Marciano. He was undefeated in forty-nine fights, including six heavyweight title defenses. With his record unmarred, Rocky retired from boxing in April, 1956 to own and operate a restaurant in Maine.

There are perhaps as many far-out tales about boxing fans, too. For instance, in 1974, Brian Brown of Wolverhampton, England, had his baby daughter christened with a name that reads like boxing's hall of fame. It includes the surnames of every world heavyweight champion from 1882 to her birth — all twenty-five of them. The wee girl, a featherweight herself, was named: Maria Sullivan Corbett Fitzsimmons Jeffries Hart Burns Johnson Willard Dempsey Tunney Schmeling Sharkey Carnera Baer Braddock Louis Charles Walcott Marciano Patterson Johansson Liston Clay Frazier Foreman Brown. If Maria ever wishes to shorten her name, she could leave out Hart. Marvin Hart held the heavyweight crown for the shortest time of all — only 235 days.

St. Bernardine taught the "art of self defense" to keep men from fighting with swords.

BOXING QUIZ

Now for some sparring with words. Just as in several other sports, some of the jargon of boxing is used in everyday language to express other meanings. How many of the boxing words and phrases with double meanings can you think of?

9

Croquet

It's an On Again, Off Again Whatchamacallit Game

Pinning down the facts about the game called *croquet* is like trying to put your finger on a flea. The game has had its ups and downs, including sideslips and several name changes.

Back in the thirteenth century, both the Italians and French were playing a game in which they knocked wooden balls around grassy areas with a curved stick. The stick looked something like the ones used in field hockey today. In French, *croc* means "hook" and *crochet* means a lot of things including "crooked stick," so either one could be the source of *croquet*, the name of the game that eventually came to North America.

But wait, in Italy they were playing a similar game; the word for "ball" was *palla* and the curved "mallet" was a *maglio*. Since words in different languages are often distant cousins, the French also gave their game the name *paile-maille*. Among other things, *maille* means a "two-handed mallet" in French. Are we all clear on that? If not, don't let it worry you, because the world has more or less settled on *croquet*, and we have even more confusion about this game to tussle with.

For instance, the claim that croquet originally was an indoor game played on a table. The argument goes that somebody who played lawn bowls (see Chapter 7) took the principle of *that* game indoors and, to make it more interesting, placed wooden arches on the table to knock the balls through. Somebody later tossed out the arches and built pockets into the table and this is said to have been the birth of *billiards*.

As might be expected, there were still players who wanted to keep the game with arches. And maybe the table game cramped their style, because they took it outdoors to the lawn and made some changes, including larger balls and arches and the use of wooden mallets. Some years later, somebody figured out it was easier to stick a bent wire in the ground than a wooden arch, so the modern wire *wicket* became standard equipment for the game.

No one is sure when croquet, or crochet, or paile-maille, crossed the English Channel to the British Isles, but it became something of a fad there. One explanation is that the game relies more on mental skill than the muscular kind, hence men and women can play together on equal footing. In 1587, when Mary Queen of Scots was on trial for the murder of her husband, Lord Darnley, her accusers pointed out that she was playing "pall mall" (as well as golf) only a few days after the crime.

In fact, the game was extremely popular among the nobility of both the British Isles and France. When Charles II was chased out of England by Oliver Cromwell in 1651, he learned the game at the royal court in France. After returning to England in 1660, he established a special grassy area in London so he and his friends could play paile-maille. This long, narrow playing field eventually became the fashionable street known as *Pall Mall*.

Despite King Charles's passion for the game, the popularity of paile-maille — or croquet — began to fade not long after he came back from France. In both countries, a new game called *lawn tennis* was catching on at the castles and manor houses, and the croquet wickets, mallets, and balls were being stored in the attic. Croquet virtually faded away at the end of the seventeenth century and didn't make a comeback until sometime in the nineteenth century. The revival of the game must have been a healthy one, because in 1861 a booklet titled *Routlege's Handbook of Croquet* was published in London. The rules laid down in this book by Edmond Routlege still serve as general guides to how the game is played.

The new enthusiasm for croquet was picked up in Ireland and Scotland, and some historians believe the game was brought to North America by Irish immigrants in about 1870. Norwich, Connecticut is singled out as the place where the game was first played in this country. As the game spread, it was adopted first by wealthy homeowners, but soon there were croquet wickets tripping up night prowlers at just about every house with a patch of lawn and in the public parks as well. Lawn tennis had come to America, too, but croquet greatly overshadowed the racquet game. In just a dozen years after its arrival in Norwich, the game had so many devotees in so many cities and towns that a national association (now called the United States Croquet Association) was formed to govern competitions.

Then history repeated itself. At the end of the century, for no apparent reason, North American fans dropped croquet like a hot potato. The collapse was the fastest ever experienced by a popular recreation craze — if you don't count Hula-Hoops™. Manufacturers and marketers of croquet sets were stuck with full warehouses.

THE BIRTH OF ROQUE

Despite the near disappearance of croquet, a few hardy souls still clung to their wickets. They felt a new variety of the game could be devised and, with a new name, become popular again. They met in Norwich, of course, and rewrote the Routlege rules to create a game similar to croquet but needing more skill. Because croquet's name was unpopular, they dropped the "c" and the "t" and arrived at a new one: *roque* (pronounced *roke*). The new game spread from the Atlantic to the Pacific, though it has never topped the charts for popularity, and croquet was restored to life in the process, waxing and waning periodically ever since.

Roque and croquet, though similar, have some significant differences. The big one is that roque is played on a hard clay area instead of on a grassy one. Both areas are called *courts*, but the roque court has its corners cut off to form an octagonal shape instead of a rectangle. A raised concrete border surrounds the roque court so that balls can be carommed off the sides, as in billiards. Roque balls are smaller and fewer than in croquet. The wickets are also smaller and number ten instead of croquet's nine. Both games have wooden stakes at the ends, which must be struck by the ball at the end of play.

Croquet is presently enjoying yet another resurgence. There were only five member clubs in the United States Croquet Association in 1977, but the number zoomed to 350 clubs in forty-eight states by 1991. About 88 percent of the Association's 5,000 members identify themselves as business people, some claiming they like the game's need for bold strategy and quick decisions — a carryover from office politics. The strategies undoubtedly work; 25 percent of the Association's members are millionaires, though machinists, construction workers, and secretaries are in there swinging mallets, too.

Croquet was included in the 1900 Olympic Games in Paris, with the Gold Medals going to the French team. But that is the only time the sport has been a part of the Olympics. In the U.S., there have been national competitions every year since 1882 (except during World War II), and presently for roque, too. Sorry, only one person from Norwich, Connecticut ever won. That was George Harland, who took the croquet crown in 1884.

The thirteenth-century French used a croc to hit the ball.

CROQUET QUIZ

Two interesting and much used phrases are derived from croquet: "to ring a bell" and "to peg out." The first is heard in everyday conversation and means that something is suddenly remembered or becomes clear to you. The second is used when stating in a slangy way that someone has died or has ended a particular task. Do you know how the two phrases were first used in croquet?

Both phrases are used in other activities, too. "Ring a bell" comes from the carnival game in which you try to ring a bell atop a tall shaft by hitting a lever with a heavy mallet. "To peg out" is a term in the game of cribbage. Think of the croquet definitions anyway.

10

Curling
A Game for all Ages

They call it "the old men's game," but don't you believe it. *Curling* is a competitive sport enjoyed by boys, girls, men, and women from junior high school age and up. High school teams vie for national championships in several countries, and men and women usually in their thirties and forties dominate the international curling competitions. That "old men" label comes from the fact that curling is one of the very few physical sports in which senior citizens aged sixty-five to ninety are actively engaged.

Another label for curling is "lawn bowls played on ice" (see lawn bowling in Chapter 7). It's true there are several ways in which the two games are alike, but there are a couple of big differences, too: 1) curling is played on a sheet of ice, and 2) the curling "balls" are round granite stones weighing forty pounds each. The smooth stones are flat on the bottom and have handles on top so that they can be sent sliding, instead of rolling, along the ice. The target is the center of a twelve-foot circle, not the small white ball used in lawn bowls. But the manner of striving to get closest to the target, as well as knocking opponents' stones away from it, is similar in both games. At least the two add up to year-round fun. One is played in summer, the other in winter.

Don't ask when or where curling first originated. Both Scotland and the Flanders region of the Netherlands claim to be the where. Some historians say the game was brought to the British Isles by Flemish immigrants in about 1428 or 1438, a rare period when England wasn't fighting with either Scotland or Flanders. Another group claims the Scots, who already played lawn bowls, simply changed the game for playing on ice when the ponds froze. Just when this happened isn't known. The earliest provable sign of curling in Scotland is a curling stone discovered when a pond was drained. "St. Js. B. Stirling 1511" is inscribed in the rock.

Both the Scots and the Flemmish claim to have invented curling.

No matter where or when the game began, the Royal Caledonian Curling Club, founded in Scotland in 1838, is recognized as the "mother" club of curlers all over the world. The game is most popular in Australia, Austria, Canada, China, England, France, Italy, New Zealand, Norway, Scotland, Sweden, Switzerland, the United States, and Wales. Scottish regiments are said to have brought curling to Canada in 1759 when they helped capture Quebec, and the first curling club was formed in Montreal in 1807. As the game spread across Canada, it also curled across the border into the United States. The first club in this country was the Orchard Lake Curling Club in Detroit, formed in 1831.

We noted earlier that a curling stone weighs forty pounds. Most of the stones, certainly all of them used in the United States and Canada, are made of granite imported from Scotland. But the game wasn't always played with these smooth, round stones. Early in the game they had square edges and sometimes blocks of wood were used. Some years ago, Canadian curlers experimented with *irons*, that is "rocks" made of cast iron. They weighed from 45 to 115 pounds and many a game ended with an aching back. Wiser heads prevailed and the forty-pound stone was standardized worldwide.

But what about that funny name, *curling*? The early Scots called a curling stone a *kuting*, and some believe the name of the game developed from this. It possibly could have come from a German word, *kurzweil*, meaning "pastime." But it's much easier to believe curling got its name because, by putting a bit of spin on it, a stone can be made to curve (or curl) around an opponent's rock and to any desired position on the ice.

A curling team is made up of four persons and is called a *rink* for some reason nobody seems to remember. The leader of the rink is called the *skip*, short for "skipper" or captain. He or she is assisted in 1, 2, 3 order by the *lead*, the first person to deliver a stone and usually the least experienced member of the rink; the *second*; and the *vice-skip* or *mate*. Each carries a *broom* to *sweep* the stones into the *house*. The latter is a twelve-foot circle marked something like an archery target.

Here's another funny word. A curling tournament is called a *bonspiel*. It's as old as the game itself and probably a Dutch word. But some believe it is a combination of the French *bon* (good) and German *spiel* (play). At least, that's what avid curlers say the game is — good play.

CURLING QUIZ

You may be a curler already or at least have seen the game played and explained on television. Then perhaps you know the meanings of the following curling terms. See how many you can get right.

Biter	In-Turn
Burned Rock	Out-Turn
Button	Sheet
Draw Weight	Shot Rock
End	Take-Out
Guard	Tee Line
Hack	Wick
Hog Line	

Both sexes and all ages use the forty-pound stones.

11

Fencing

It's Dueling without Playing for Keeps

In Great Britain, they spell the word "defense" with a "c" instead of an "s". That's how we get their word "defence" and, when it's shortened, the name of the sport *to fence* or *fencing*. It's another example of physical recreation with its name and skills handed down from warfare. When gunpowder came into use and shooting guns took the place of swordsmanship, men continued to carry light swords for protection and as a fashionable adornment.

Unfortunately, some chaps were all too prone to use their swords, and many duels were fought in the centuries before the bloody squabbling was made illegal in civilized countries. However, if a fellow figured he might have to fight a duel some day, he needed to develop sword skills. So, fencing schools and fencing masters appeared. And from these, in turn, dueling was developed into a recreation instead of playing for keeps.

Of course, swordplay, if you can call it play, existed long before the Christian era. The oldest known sword is a short bronze one found in the tomb of Saragon, a King of Ur who lived about 5,000 years ago. Personal duels, the kind you read about in novels and see in old Zorro movies, didn't come along until the twelfth or thirteenth centuries. At first, the combatants fought until one was killed. But, then, somebody figured his honor would be fully satisfied if he only nicked the other guy instead of skewering him in the gizzard. Thus, a more gentlemanly duel with swords became the fashion.

Several European countries lay claim to the idea of non-fatal dueling with swords and then turning this practice into a sport. Germany has a strong claim. The *Marxbruder* (Fencing) *Guild of Lowenberg* existed there in 1383, and a manuscript dated in 1410 described the sport and the use of blunt-ended swords. The Germans fenced with a heavy, clumsy sword thirty-two to thirty-six inches long with no hand guard. What may be the first booklet about fencing was published by Achille Marozzo of Italy in 1536. Even Camillo Agrippa of Milan, a noted engineer and mathematician, got in on the act. While in Rome in 1553, he wrote a book titled *A Treatise on the Science of Arms* and dealt with fencing in detail. The famous artist Michaelangelo drew the illustrations for it.

Fencing schools and fencing masters were a no-no in England for some time in the 1400s because they were "enticing sons of respectable persons to waste time and spend the property of their parents in bad practices." But the sport obviously became tolerated, because in 1599 a man named Silver published *Brief Introductions on My Paradoxes of Defence*.

A Polish nobleman, Count Koenigsmarken, is said to have developed the design for the modern fencing *foil*, back in about

The first duels (with rules) were held in the twelfth century.

Fencing is a friendly way of competing with swords.

1680. But we owe it to Henri Saint-Didier, a Frenchman, for having coined the names of just about everything related to fencing. He gave them names in 1570, and most of them are still in use. For example: *épée*, the French word for "sword", *sabre*, *en-garde*, *disengage*, *coupe*, *double*, *dedoublement*, and *priz-de-fer*. *Foil*, mentioned earlier, is an English word and apparently comes from the fact that the sword is largely used to "foil" an opponent's thrusts.

The foil, épée, and sabre (or saber) are the three types of swords now used in fencing competition. The foil and épée appear about the same, though the épée is slightly heavier and has a larger hand guard. The sabre weighs the same as the foil and has a hand guard similar to a traditional cavalry sword. The difference in fencing with the three weapons is the area of the fencer's body that can be used as a target.

Fencing was there when the Olympic Games were revived in 1896, with competition with all three types of swords. Women's fencing was introduced at the Games in 1924. They compete only with foils. Then, as now, Europeans dominate the sport, though Cuban fencers have won a number of Gold Medals. The sport hasn't a great many devotees in the United States and Canada. But they make up in enthusiasm what they lack in numbers. Several colleges and universities—and even some high schools—include fencing in their athletic programs.

FENCING QUIZ

Now try the pen versus the sword. Dueling, the "for keeps" ancestor of fencing, has been a frequent subject of literature. Shakespeare's Hamlet fought a famous stage duel. Robert Sheridan, the Irish playwright and a noted duelist himself, nevertheless ridiculed the practice in his play, *The Rivals*. Name the following:

Who was Hamlet's dueling opponent?
Who were the duelists in *The Rivals*?

12

Football

What You Call it Depends on What You Play

Back in the year 50 A.D., Li Yu, a Chinese poet, wrote of a game in which "the ball goes flying across like the moon." Was this an early version of the soccer football we know today? It could be. The Chinese character he used for the name of the game means "football."

As a sportswriter, Li Yu was late for the kickoff. Football in one form or another had already been popular for more than a thousand years. Hairy-chested Chinese played a bruising game called *tsu chu*, which translates to mean "kick a leather ball with the foot." Spartans played *episkyros*, which means "team game." The early Greeks called it *sphennida* and used an inflated goatskin ball. The Aztecs in South America played it as *ullamaliztli*, kicking around a ball made of a local product that we now call rubber. Centuries later, when the Pilgrims landed on this side of the Atlantic, they were astonished to find the Indians kicking a deerskin ball around in a game called (take a deep breath) *pasuckquakkohowoq*. It means "gather to play football."

The ancient Romans played a rough-and-tumble game called *harpastum*, which means "stealing." It called for a lot of running, kicking, tripping, and elbowing. Nevertheless, Augustus Caesar, who lived from 63 B.C. to 14 A.D. and was Number 1 honcho in Rome, thought the game was "too gentle" for keeping the troops fit for fighting, and he banned it.

Since soldiers have always had ways of getting around the orders of the brass, the legions never fully gave up football. In fact, it may have been the Roman troops who introduced the sport into the British Isles, where it scored an even bigger success.

One account in the year 217 A.D. tells us that boys played a ball-kicking game in the streets of Chester, England using the skull of a defeated Dane as a ball. For lack of a better name, they called their sport *kicking the Dane's head*. The lads in Derby and other towns are also known to have been playing a form of football at this time, usually in celebration of the defeat of Roman cohorts in local skirmishes. But they probably used a more sportsmanlike ball.

Young men caught playing "unprofitabill sportes" landed in jail.

SOCCER

These days the players and fans only scream for the heads of the officials or the opposing team, but some claim the gruesome Chester pastime was the origin of *soccer football* as we know it today. Whether that's true or not, it was soon apparent that football would become the British national sport. Rivalries grew between towns and villages, and games were played as frequently as possible, weather permitting. Eventually Shrove Tuesday marked the date of the largest annual football matches. Every able-bodied male in a town, sometimes a hundred or more, would turn out to challenge the team of a neighboring town.

There were few rules and hardly any limit to the playing area. An inflated cow's bladder was dropped midway between the rival communities, and the team that kicked it into the center of the opposing team's town was the victor. Since the wide-ranging mob often flattened hedges, trampled gardens, and scattered livestock, the town fathers called a halt and ordered the players to confine their sport to vacant areas or stop playing. The result was the beginning of standard rules, goal lines, and a fixed number of players on each team.

As football fever spread across the British Isles, various spoil-sport kings and at least one queen tried to curb the game. They said it was bad for the morals and a threat to national defense, because you can't train with a longbow or pikestaff when you're out in the pasture kicking a ball around. Anyone caught playing football, or letting a game be played on his land, was clapped into prison.

Henry II probably was the first to put his foot down. Then, in 1314, Edward II issued another proclamation forbidding football because it was disturbing the peace. "There is a great noise in the city," declared the king, "caused by hustling over large balls from which many evils might arise."

His successor, Edward III, as well as Richard II, Henry III, Henry IV, and Henry VIII, ordered a stop to football on the grounds that it took up the time of young men who ought to be practicing archery, a skill needed in the military service. Two of the kings also banned golf and tennis in the bargain.

Nobody seemed to pay much attention, because in 1572 Queen Elizabeth I had to proclaim all over again that "no foteballe be used or suffered within the city of London and the liberties thereof upon pain of imprisonment."

Earlier in Scotland, Kings James II and James III had banned "footballe and golfe." And in 1491, James IV issued yet another proclamation that said "in na place of realme thair be usit fut-ballis, golfe or other sic unprofitabill sportes."

His majesty wasn't very good at enforcing the rule, because six years later his royal treasurer recorded a payment of two shillings for "fut balles." Apparently the royal court spent more time playing football than learning how to spell it.

Despite the outward appearance of royal disapproval, football never lost its appeal. Players and fans turned out in droves at every opportunity, and the game just couldn't be put down. Early in the sixteenth century, the Irish, ever ready to defy the English crown, devised a Gaelic version of football, called *hurling*, and played it openly. This emboldened the English and Scots to defy the bans, too, though they did it more furtively than the Irish.

But it was not until James I was crowned in 1603 that the game emerged fully into the open. By that time guns and gunpowder had replaced the longbow as the basic military weapon and there was no need for long hours of practice on the archery range. The king not only approved of football, he encouraged it. Even the puritanical Oliver Cromwell, who took over the reins in 1649, was an enthusiastic football player in his spare time. He saw no chance that the game would endanger his Christian morals. By the end of the eighteenth century, football was so popular in Scotland that fishwives were playing it. On Shrove Tuesdays there were annual matches between married and unmarried teams in which the married fishwives usually won. They called the game *melleys*, which probably comes from the old English words *mell* and *melee*, meaning a mixed fight or a skirmish. It figures.

Up to now, we've been talking about a form of football that is almost entirely a kicking game. No player is permitted to lay hands on the ball except the goalkeeper. In order to know how this type

Soccer is a very emotional game, especially for the spectators.

of game came to be known as *soccer*, you have to first understand how *rugby football* came to be.

RUGBY

Rugby football is entirely an English invention, and an embarrassing accident at that. It happened one afternoon in 1823 when a student named William Ellis was playing in a kicking-type football game at Rugby College. He muffed a kick and, frustrated and chagrined that he had missed the ball, picked it up in his arms and ran down the field with it.

Horrors! That just isn't done, old chap. The team captain apologized to the opposition for the breach of etiquette, and Ellis was roundly criticized by his teammates.

The news got around, of course. Students at other colleges thought there might be something in this new kicking-running type of game after all. By 1839, at Cambridge they were seriously playing what they called "that game at Rugby" or simply "Rugby's game." A Cambridge student, Arthur Pell, wrote the first set of rules in which it was permitted to run with the ball if it was caught on the fly or on the first bounce. Of course, if you run with the ball there has to be some way to stop you. So, the *tackle* was invented.

Other schools tried the game and liked it. By the time Rugby College got around to adopting its own invention in 1841, the game was already known as *rugby*. It was strictly an intramural sport until 1873. In that year, Charterhouse and Westminster met for the first intercollegiate rugby game. Westminster won. The game was already being played in France, and in the early 1870s it was picked up by students at McGill University in Montreal. McGill players took it to the United States.

Years later a small monument was erected on the Rugby College campus. The inscription reads:

THIS STONE
COMMEMORATES THE EXPLOIT OF
WILLIAM WEBB ELLIS
WHO WITH A FINE DISREGARD FOR THE RULES OF
FOOTBALL AS PLAYED IN HIS TIME,
FIRST TOOK THE BALL IN HIS ARMS AND RAN WITH IT,
THUS ORIGINATING THE DISTINCTIVE FEATURE OF
THE RUGBY GAME
A.D. 1823

Rugby, the happy accident, broke another tradition in the development of sports. Instead of being a popular public game that college students picked up and ran with, rugby was first developed on college campuses, then adopted by amateurs and professionals on public playing fields.

As you might expect, there was warm rivalry between the town teams. A feud also arose between the two popular types of football ... the rugby game and the kicking-only game that stemmed back to that unlucky Dane who lost his head at Chester. Heated debates were held regarding running, kicking, and handling the ball. Finally, in 1863, a group favoring the kicking game formed England's Football Association and adopted a set of game rules that drew the line between rugby football and *association football*. The new organization allowed players to run and kick to their heart's desire, but only the goalkeepers could put their hands on the ball. Most body contact with opponents was ruled out.

Rugby had been nicknamed *rugger*, and players and fans soon shortened the name of association football to *assoc*. But it was a fellow named Charles Wreford-Brown, an association player and committee member, who coined the word *soccer*. Asked if he'd like to play a game of rugger, he gave a twist to assoc and said, "No, soccer." The name caught on, but, strangely, not on his home ground. Only in the United States and Canada is the association form of the game called soccer. In England and elsewhere in the world it's simply called football. But whether you call it football, soccer, or kicking the Dane's head, the soccer-type game is the most popular and heavily-attended sport in the world.

Soccer is far and away the most fanatical game in the world, too. Fans get so excited, especially at international matches, that fistfights, gunshots, riots, and other forms of mayhem are common. Spectators periodically are trampled to death by surging crowds or crushed in collapsing grandstands. In January of 1991, more than forty people died in Johannesburg, South Africa when a brawl broke out between fans of rival teams. Europe has witnessed several such catastrophes, and on one occasion in Peru as many as 300 people died in a riot that began simply because the fans didn't like a referee's ruling. In Rio de Janeiro, stadium officials had to dig a ditch seven feet wide and five feet deep around the soccer field and fill the ditch with water to keep angry fans from the referees and players. In Glasgow, Scotland, the canny and cautious Scots regularly field as many stretcher bearers and ambulance drivers as there are players in the game.

Nor is all the mayhem in the stadium. When England lost to West Germany during the 1990 World Cup games in Italy, soccer fans rioted in thirty English towns. Three people died and scores were injured in the violence. More than 600 rioters landed in jail.

A big reason for the international enthusiasm for soccer is that the rules are so simple, teams can get along without knowing their opponent's language. Even the fans can understand what a foreign referee is signaling … though they might disagree and scream curses at him in another language.

A reason the kicking game is growing in popularity among schools in the United States and Canada is that it needs very little equipment and muscle compared to rugby and American or Canadian football. You don't have to be a 200-pounder or more than six feet tall to make the team. Boys and girls of average weight and in good physical condition can play soccer with comparatively small risk of serious injury.

Soccer is a game in which players use their heads.

AMERICAN AND CANADIAN FOOTBALL _____

Football in its rugby and soccer versions didn't catch on in America until the early part of the nineteenth century. It came in two ways. Universities and colleges on this side of the Atlantic adopted the games from schools in England and Scotland. As public sports, both amateur and professional, the games were gradually introduced by immigrants from England, Scotland, and Ireland.

By 1866, soccer was well enough established as a public sport that an all-star team from the New Jersey area went to Montreal to play three games with an all-star team there. The following year, the Canadians visited New Jersey. The teams must have been evenly matched. Each had two wins, two losses, and two draws in the six-game series.

Meanwhile, developments were happening on university playing fields. Harvard students were playing the soccer-style game until the faculty banned it in 1860 for reasons now obscure. For some years the student body stuck to their books. But finally, in 1871, frustrated by the ban on soccer, they did an end run around the faculty by devising a brand-new and different game. They called it the *Boston game* and it combined features of both soccer and rugby. It was still more kicking than running and tackling, but the rugby-style drop-kick, free kick, offside, and oval ball were written into the rules. Thus the seeds were sown for what we know today as *American football*. (Incidentally, despite the kind of inflated bladder football players may have kicked around in early times, the so-called *pigskin* that sportswriters like to write about is not really a pig's skin. The ball is pebbled steer leather and weighs just one or two ounces short of a pound when inflated.)

Other schools didn't care very much for Harvard's new game, though Princeton and Rutgers played the first intercollegiate game in America on November 6, 1869. At the time, the Princeton team decided to be their own cheering section and let loose with bloodcurdling screams as they played. The idea was to scare the Rutgers players so much they would be off their game. It didn't work. The Princeton players got themselves so confused and short of breath by their own yelling that they lost the game, 6-4.

Meanwhile, Harvard players, discouraged that other schools didn't adopt their new game, began scouting elsewhere for opponents. While they were looking, an invitation came from Montreal's McGill University to play rugby. Thus it was arranged that two games would be played in the spring of 1874 on Harvard's field at Cambridge and one would be played in the fall in Montreal. The first game in Cambridge would be played by Harvard's "Boston" rules, the second by McGill's rugby rules. Harvard won the first 3-0, and the second game was played to a scoreless tie.

Quite accidentally, this meeting established an important basic feature of American football. It had been agreed that the Harvard and McGill teams would play with fifteen men on each side. But when McGill travelled to Cambridge, four of the Canadian players couldn't make the trip. It was quickly arranged to play with eleven men per team, a feature of American football ever since in both amateur and professional play. When the Canadians adopted the game, they established rules much like the American version. But in *Canadian football*, each team has twelve players on the field and the playing field is ten yards longer.

Many rule changes and additions have been adopted as American and Canadian football have expanded in collegiate and public rivalries. Quarterbacks first appeared in 1880, along with a substitution of scrimmage for the rugby scrum. Downs became a part of the game in 1882. The Australians developed their version of the game, too, taking what they liked mainly of the Gaelic game called hurling, imported by Irish gold miners, and adding a bit of rugby in the bargain. The Aussies call their game *footy* and it's a fast, freewheeling game that calls for much skill and inventiveness on the part of every player. Players can both pass and kick while running with the ball. Footy can be bruising, too, but no padding is worn.

Today in North America there is also a six-man version of football. It was developed for teams that like a fast-paced passing game and for schools that lack the money and muscle to compete against eleven-man teams.

Incidentally, despite international soccer fever and the popularity of American, Canadian, and Australian football, good old rough-and-ready rugby is the preferred national sport of New Zealand. Rugby was included in the Olympic games four times between 1900 and 1924, but soccer is the only form of football included in Olympic competition today. Recent studies show that in the United States soccer is the third most popular sport among teenagers. Only basketball and volleyball attract more players. In Canada, more schoolboys now play soccer than their national sport, hockey.

So, if you mention football, you'd better make it clear which kind you're talking about — soccer; rugby; American, Canadian, or Australian football; or the six-man sport. Otherwise, you can get confused quicker than you can say *pasuckquakkohowoq*.

SOCCER QUIZ

Many soccer terms are found in other sports, too. Can you name the other sports (often more than one) in which the following terms are used?

Boarding	Kill a Penalty
Charging	Open Net
Crease	Offside
Dribble	Penalty Box
Hack	Pitch
Hat Trick	Pyramid
Interference	Scissors Kick
Jockeying	Sweeper
Kick-Off	

Make copies of this quiz and try it on your friends. You could become the neighborhood soccer guru.

13

Golf

Give the Scots Credit for this One

The place of *golf's* origin, like the birth of many games, was disputed for centuries. Holland and Scotland made strong claims, though club-and-ball games were known in several countries as far back as the pre-Christian era. The ancient Romans knocked a hard ball about with a club, but they abandoned the sport in favor of other, tougher ones.

Centuries later, when the French were playing the game that became croquet (see Chapter 9), somebody experimented with a cross-country version of that. They'd pick a distant target, perhaps a church or a barn door, and hammer wooden balls toward it. Could that have been the start of golf?

The Dutch claim to the game was strengthened by the name itself. *Golf*, they said, comes from the Low Dutch word *kolf*, which means "club." They also used *colf*, *colven*, and *kolven*. But then there's the German *kolbe* and the Scandinavian *qouffe*, which mean "club," too. The word and the game could have been brought along by the Danes when they invaded the British Isles in 1003. Finally, there's the old Scottish word *goulf*, which means "strike" or "cuff." Even the Scots called the game variously *goff* and *gowf* before settling on the present name.

Despite this wordy puzzle, additional clues now lead historians to agree that golf, as it is played today, originated on the eastern shore of Scotland. In fact, the Scots called the rolling stretches of shoreland *links*, a word now applied to golf courses. Another

Scottish word, *divot*, means "piece of turf," as any duffer can tell you.

The most likely story of how the game started, golf historians believe, is that in some ancient time Scottish shepherds became bored sitting out on hillsides with no one to talk to but flocks of sheep. So, to break the monotony, they used their crooked sticks to knock pebbles around. To make a game of this knock-about diversion, they dug small holes and aimed the pebbles at them.

It's a good story and generally accepted. But it doesn't explain how, when golf became popular all over the British Isles, the game was taken over by people a lot higher on the social ladder than poor shepherds. At least in the early development of the game, it was played mainly by royalty and the well-to-do. Only in the present century has golf become a game for just about everyone.

In any event, golf was extremely popular in Scotland and England long before Columbus discovered America. So much so that a circular portion of the great stained glass east window of Gloucester Cathedral, built in the 1300s, shows a golfer swinging

Scottish shepherds are said to have started golfing on the "links."

his club at a ball. By 1457, the game had become such a fad that King James II told the Scottish parliament to issue an edict banning all golf, as well as football, because they interfered with the compulsory archery practice needed for national defense. When many men still found time to play golf after archery practice, the king, a canny Scot, simply lengthened the hours required with the bow and arrows.

But wait! Despite the constant threat of invasion and the need to concentrate on archery, even the king himself can become hooked on golf. James IV of Scotland was a fair-to-middling player. But in 1491 he, too, had to decree: "... that in na place in tha realme thair be usit fut-ballis, golf or other sic unprofitabill sportis." But royalty has privileges. The king ignored his own decree and kept on playing golf. His son, James V, was not so hot on the game, but he relaxed the rules against playing it. His daughter, Mary, learned golf as a girl and is the first woman golfer of record. She took her enthusiasm for the game with her when she was educated in France and on her return continued to call the boy who carried her clubs by the French term *cadet*, pronounced "cad-day." The Scots and English, as usual, mispronounced and misspelled the French word, and our modern word *caddie* is the result.

When Mary became Queen of Scotland in 1542, she continued to play golf and gave the nod to ordinary citizens who wanted to play. It was in her reign, in 1552, that the world-famous golf course at St. Andrews, Scotland was established. Much later, two years before the start of the American Revolution, the "Royal and Ancient Golf Club of St. Andrews" was founded. It's named for the patron saint of Scotland.

English rulers were not so tolerant of the game. Several of them, including Henry VIII and Queen Elizabeth, banned golf and football altogether. But with the union of Scotland and England in 1603, when fun-loving James VI of Scotland became King James I of both, he took an entourage of golf players with him to London, and the lid was off.

Just how golf made the trip to North America is anybody's guess. But some assume that it was brought here by officers and crew of the British navy. As early as 1795, there were notices in Georgia and North Carolina newspapers of club meetings and annual balls. It is known that there were three-hole golf courses at Montreal and Quebec in the 1850s, and the first organized golf club in Canada was the Royal Montreal Golf Club, formed November 4, 1873.

The first golf club in the United States is said to have been the St. Andrews Golf Club of Yonkers, New York, founded by five men on November 14, 1888. But this claim is disputed by golf clubs in Foxburg, Pennsylvania and Sarasota, Florida, who say they were founded in 1887 and 1886, respectively. The Yonkers golfers are the best documented, however. Their first course was a three-hole layout in a cow pasture owned by John Reid, one of the five club members. Then the group moved to an apple orchard nearby, where they became known as the "Apple Tree Gang," and, following yet another move, finally wound up in Mount Hope, New York, where the club remains today.

You wouldn't think it today, but in the early days of golf, women weren't welcome on the courses, despite the example set by Mary Queen of Scots. Women's lib prevailed in the nineteenth century, though. A female golf club was organized at St. Andrews, Scotland in 1867, though the ladies were restricted to the putting green. The following year, they convinced the male chauvinist golfers that they should be allowed to play the whole course — and have been there ever since. The ladies had still another problem. At the outset, women's fashions put a damper on their game. Bustles, bonnets, corsets, and full, flowing skirts made putting and swinging a club very difficult, especially in a brisk wind. Undeterred, some women golfers took to wearing elastic rubber bands around their waists. When the wind started blowing, they pushed the bands down around their knees so ballooning skirts wouldn't hamper their style — golf-wise that is. Female golf fashions were freed up following World War I.

In North America, as in its early days in Europe, golf was considered a "rich man's hobby" until 1913. That year Francis O. Duimet, a twenty-year-old former caddie, won the United States Open tournament at Brookline, Massachusetts. Suddenly people realized they didn't have to be wealthy to be golfers, and they started flocking to public and private courses. Today golfers in the United States and Canada number in the millions, partly because more and more girls and women are teeing off. In 1990, the National Golf Foundation reported that in the United States 87 percent of the golfers were male, but 41 percent of the *new* golfers were female.

You don't have to be an adult to be a great golfer, either. In 1968, Tommy Moore of Hagerstown, Maryland sank a hole-in-one on the 145-yard fourth hole at the Woodbrier Golf Course in

On windy days, ladies wore rubber bands around their skirts.

Martinsburg, West Virginia. Tommy was just a month over six years old. The odds against sinking a hole-in-one on an eighteen-hole golf course are 11,000 to 1.

You doubt the kid did it? Later in the same year Tommy sank another hole-in-one. So there!

The Apple Tree Gang formed America's first golf club in Yonkers.

GOLF QUIZ

Golf widow is a slang term for a lady whose husband spends all his spare time on the golf course. She says the game is for the birds. Avid golfers might agree — but for a different reason. Their jargon is filled with bird terms. How many of these can you define?

Albatross	Eagle
Bird Dog	Double Eagle
Birdie	Quail High
Buzzard	Round Robin

14

Gymnastics
Strength, Skill, and Grace —
but Little Publicity

Don't look now, but the word *gymnastics* comes from the Greek word *gymna-zein*, which means "to exercise while naked." And an outdoor *gymnasium* is where the ancient Greeks used to work up a sweat in their birthday suits.

It wasn't all fun and games. In those days, physical fitness was a big part of every male's education. Every city and town did its darndest to develop top Olympic athletes as well as condition men for the army. Boys and young men were required to report every day for physical training, which then also included boxing, wrestling, and track and field events. Huge buildings (gymnasiums) were built for this purpose. Some were so large there was room inside for running tracks and space for throwing javelins and discuses. The better ones had dressing rooms (or more likely "undressing" rooms), baths, and lecture rooms. The walls often were decorated with murals and statues.

Since the young men spent the better part of a day at the gymnasiums, the city fathers also provided shade trees, benches, and walks around the buildings where they could relax their sore muscles. Admiring girls, the world's first "groupies," were attracted to these shady places, and then elder citizens. Thus, the concept of today's public parks and picnic grounds emerged.

When the Romans conquered the Greeks, they adopted the gymnastics idea and took it back to Italy for the training of their legionnaires. In the meantime, the Greeks had become more modest and were exercising with their clothes on. The Romans followed suit. But, alas, it was the Romans who let the ancient Olympic Games decline, then come to an end. And in 392 A.D., Emperor Theodosius abolished compulsory physical training and closed the gymnasiums.

The buildings weren't boarded up and abandoned, however. Learned men, wiser than the emperor, took over the gymnasiums and turned them into centers for learning the arts and sciences. Today, we'd call them the local schoolhouse.

Without government backing, the physical training programs — even public interest in gymnastics — faded out. The interest wasn't revived for another seven or eight centuries. Accounts

The original "gymna-zein" was a place "to exercise while naked."

written in England in the 1100s mention open areas established for the purpose of running, jumping, and throwing. This sounds like track and field events, but we'll deal with this in a later chapter because when gymnastics finally did make a comeback, sports like boxing, wrestling, weight lifting, and track and field events had been separated from them.

The true gymnastics as we presently see them got their new lease on life principally in Sweden, Germany, and Czechoslovakia in the early 1800s. Each country developed its own type of program, and the best features of each have been adapted and improved to make up modern competition. For example, a German, Friedrich Ludwig Jahn, is credited with creating at least three pieces of modern gymnastic apparatus — the horizontal bar, the parallel bars, and the rings.

An interesting sidelight on this revival of the sport occurred in France. Jules Leotard, a gymnast who turned professional acrobat, invented a one-piece, body-clinging exercise costume for himself that now bears his name. Jules urged other men to wear it, saying: "Don't you want to be adored by the ladies?" But the ladies adored the *leotard*, too, and adopted the garment for themselves.

Incidentally, never call a gymnast an acrobat, especially if he has bigger muscles than you. A gymnast is a skilled amateur who trains and competes for the love of it. Acrobats are professional showpeople who can make simple feats look more difficult than they really are. Gymnastics require strength, grace, and skill, plus rigid physical and mental discipline. Some adaptations are used as preventive and corrective therapy in cases of wounds, accidents, and diseases such as polio and cerebral palsy. Yet the sport of gymnastics is the least known, least publicized major sport in the world. You can check this out by scanning your local sports pages.

Girls engaged in gymnastics might prefer to call their efforts *calisthenics*. It's from two Greek words: *kallos*, meaning "beauty," and *sthenos*, meaning "strength." In other words, they exercise for beauty, and who doesn't agree with that?

Gymnastics were brought to America in the 1800s, mainly by German and Czech immigrants. Since there was no organized sport of the kind in North America, they formed clubs of their own. These were eventually broadened to include anybody interested in gymnastics. Records of the Amateur Athletic Union, which governs the sport in this country, list gymnastic champions back to 1885. As a matter of course, colleges and high schools began teaching gymnastics in their physical education programs, bringing the sport full circle back to its ancient Greek beginnings. The University of Illinois had the first college team.

Today, despite a lack of sports page coverage, gymnastics are a thriving international sport. They were included in the first modern Olympic Games at Athens in 1896, and female gymnasts were included in 1928 (with their clothes on, of course). A worldwide organization, Federation Internationale de Gymnastique (FIG), now governs the sport. A check of Olympic records bears out this international interest by revealing the wide assortment of countries that have captured individual and team Gold Medals.

GYMNASTICS QUIZ

Exercise your brain with this. In the modern Olympics, the following gymnastic equipment is used: *long horse, pommel horse, horizontal bar, parallel bars, uneven bars, horizontal beam,* and *stationary rings.*

1. Which of these are used by female competitors?
2. Which are not used by male competitors?

German and Czech immigrants brought gymnastics to America.

15

Handball

A Teenager Brought it to America

You'll have to hand it to the Irish for inventing this game. As usual, the Romans are said to have played a game of the sort in ancient times, but the lads in the land of shamrocks devised our present handball game at some time in the tenth century. They called it *game of fives* or simply *fives*, because all the fingers of the hand were used to bat a small ball against a wall. It was several hundred years later that the term *handball* came into use.

The game gravitated slowly through the rest of the British Isles, making little progress except in Ireland until the 1800s. Then some outstanding handball stars appeared, and people began to take more notice of the game. In the forefront of this growing popularity was Meham Baggs. He developed what he called "screw tosses," with which he made the ball rebound from the wall with a spin, a curve, a dip, or other erratic ways. Rival players soon copied Baggs's bag of tricks, and handball became a more exciting game with more players and fans.

A young rising star in the 1870s was sixteen-year-old Phil Casey. He emigrated from Ireland to Brooklyn, New York in 1882, bringing a few of his favorite handballs with him. But in New York there was no place to play the game, and nobody to play it except a few idle Irish immigrants like himself. Casey was not to be denied. He built a handball court, got his cronies as well as the neighbors interested in the game, then started building more courts and opened a handball school in the bargain.

In the tenth century, the Irish called handball the Game of Fives.

All the while the enterprising Casey was taking on all challengers and beating them handily. One of these was Bernard McQuade, another Irishman living in New York. In 1888, McQuade boasted he was a better man with a handball than Casey, and dared the latter to meet him in a tournament for the "American championship." No sooner said than done. Casey quickly defeated McQuade, then decided he could win the world crown by challenging John Lawlor, the Irish handball champion.

The plan for the tourney was to play ten games in Cork, Ireland, then meet in New York until one player won eleven games. A side bet of $1,000 made things worthwhile. Challenger Casey didn't do so well in Cork. He won only four of the ten games. But when back on home ground in New York, he won seven straight and became the first World Champion of handball. After that Casey continued to boost his reputation and bank account by taking on all comers. He retired from handball undefeated in 1900. His legacy was an awareness of handball all across the continent. Students who trained at Casey's New York school scattered to other locations, and soon handball courts were established in every major city in the United States and Canada.

A curious change for the better took place in the sport at this time. Phil Casey and those he played against were "pros." Their main reason for playing handball was money — side bets made before the games. With its dynamic champion in retirement, professional handball went into a decline in North America. Meanwhile, amateurs were getting a handle on the game. They were attracted to the new handball courts springing up around the nation and liked the game so much that three years before the Mighty Casey retired, the Amateur Athletic Union moved in and staged a national handball tournament. Michael Eagan of Jersey City, New Jersey was the first champion. You guessed it, he was born in Galway, Ireland.

Two people vie with each other in handball, or four can play a "doubles" game, as in tennis. The game Baggs, Casey, Eagan, and all the others played was *four-wall* handball, the original form of the game and one of two versions now played. In this form, the players are completely surrounded by walls and the ball can be played off any one of them and the ceiling as well. The other version, *one-wall* handball, made its debut in 1913 on bathing beaches near New York City, and the rules of the game were altered for this type of play. One-wall courts, being easier and cheaper to erect, soon were installed in schoolyards and public parks from coast to coast. Today hardly a YMCA or YWCA, health-club, or school gym is without the markings for a four-wall or one-wall handball court.

Girls were slow in taking to handball, but not any more. Today bevies of female players are on the courts, for enjoyment and because the game is great for physical fitness.

HANDBALL QUIZ

Team handball, also known as *field handball,* was included in the 1972 Olympic Games and again in 1976, but was dropped after that. Can you describe how team handball differs from the four-wall and one-wall games?

Phil Casey brought handball to Brooklyn, New York in 1882.

16

Hockey

It's Said to be the Fastest Game on Earth

This chapter is about *ice hockey*. The game is patterned after *field hockey*, an older game, which you can learn more about in Chapter 25. We'll have to take it for granted that men in England played, or at least closely watched, field hockey in the mid-1800s, because they knew all about it when they came to Canada and started playing the game on ice.

As the story goes, in 1855 soldiers of Her Majesty's Royal Canadian Rifles, a British regiment stationed at Kingston, Ontario, took advantage of smooth ice on the frozen harbor and began a game similar to field hockey. Whether or not the players wore ice skates at the time is not recorded, but the game was the birth of modern ice hockey.

Like so many such stories, this one is disputed by regional historians in Montreal and Halifax, Nova Scotia. Each city claims British soldiers stationed there played ice hockey earlier than 1855. To counter these claims, it has even been suggested that a free-wheeling *shinny* was played on the Kingston ice in about 1830. This may be true, because early explorers reported seeing Canadian Indians with curved sticks chasing small balls about on frozen lakes and rivers. In fact, some believe the game's name is an adaptation of an Indian howl of pain. When accidentally (or purposely) hit by a stick, an Indian would yell *ho-ghee*, meaning "It hurts!" Hence, the name *hockey*. Another, more likely, theory is that French Canadians dubbed the game *hoquet*, after the French word for a shepherd's crook, which the hockey stick resembled. This was later Anglicized to *hockey*.

Despite the claims and counterclaims as to hockey's place of origin, Montreal steadfastly maintains that the first "true" ice hockey was played there by students of McGill University in 1875. Halifax sports fans snicker at this claim, because it was a Halifax student, J.G.A. Creighton, who brought the game to McGill. In any event, the first set of hockey rules was written at McGill in 1875, and female students at the university were playing the game in 1894 and possibly earlier. 1893 is believed to be the year ice hockey

Lord Stanley of Preston, Governor General of Canada, donated the Stanley Cup in 1893.

was introduced in the United States by students at Yale and at Johns Hopkins University in Baltimore. They had witnessed games in Montreal and brought the rules home with them.

The *Stanley Cup*, which is as prized in hockey as the World Series pennant is in baseball, goes to the National Hockey League team that wins a postseason playoff series, which is limited to the season's four top teams. It was put up by Lord Stanley of Preston, Governor General of Canada, for the 1893-94 season. He directed that the cup should be awarded to the Montreal Amateur Athletic Association champion. His Lordship was away in England by the time the Montreal AAA team defeated the Capitals, a team from Ottawa, and captured the cup. Lord Stanley had coughed up ten pounds sterling ($48.66) for the tall silver cup. The original is now on display in the Hockey Hall of Fame in Toronto.

As you've noticed, the Stanley Cup was originally intended for amateur hockey champions. Oddly, the competition for it gave a boost to professional hockey, and, by a process of osmosis, the cup eventually became the prized possession of the pros. As hockey fever spread across Canada, towns vied with each other to attract the best players so they could win the Stanley Cup. This meant luring players from other teams by paying them under-the-table money. By the time the National Hockey League was formed in 1909, the payments were being made openly and the so-called amateurs were full-scale professionals. Play for the Stanley Cup has been a feature of the NHL ever since.

Naturally, early ice hockey was played on frozen rinks out-of-doors in winter. (The first historical reference to skating on ice goes back to 1015 in Holland, and the word *skates* comes from the Dutch *schaats*.) But skaters in England enjoyed an indoor rink with artificial ice as early as 1876. Three years later there was indoor skating at Madison Square Garden in New York, and the following year at the St. Nicholas Arena, where a four-team hockey league took to the ice. Canada's first artificial ice rinks were opened in Vancouver and Victoria, British Columbia in 1911.

Speaking of indoor hockey rinks, the angry owner of one of them is said to have invented the hockey puck. In the early days of the game, a lacrosse ball (see next chapter) was used, or even the kneecap of a cow. Very often, however, a wooden ball was the "puck," and it was almost impossible to control. When the game moved indoors to artificial ice this became a problem because the wildly ricocheting ball often crashed through the arena windows.

One owner, whose name is long since forgotten, became fed up one day after suffering several hundred dollars in damage. He grabbed the ball and, with his pocketknife, carved off the top and bottom. Voila! He had invented the puck. Today it is made of hard rubber and its regulation size is 2.54 centimeters (1 inch) thick and 7.62 centimeters (3 inches) in diameter. On average, an NHL team uses about 10,000 pucks in play and practice during a season. The word *puck*, incidentally, first was used in hockey in 1891. It comes from an English dialect word meaning to "poke" or "hit."

Until the NHL made six-man teams official in 1912, there was a seventh man, called the *rover*, on each team. He played both offense and defense. The rover was dropped under new NHL rules, but some western teams kept him on the ice until 1922. Before 1900, there were no substitutions in a game. All players skated for the full sixty minutes. If a player was injured, the other team had to drop a man. These days, as you know, hockey is the only game in which substitutions are made while play continues, a big reason why ice hockey is said to be "the fastest game in the world." Talk about speed! Some years ago Bobby Hull, while playing with the Chicago Black Hawks, made a slap shot measured at 118.3 miles-per-hour.

Another rule that became outdated was an early one that said the goaltender had to remain standing throughout a game. If he went down on the ice, he was fined or sent to the penalty box, or both. The rule was tossed out, along with one that bothered the hockey referee. Until 1914, referees had to put the puck right down on the ice for a face-off. They got so many mashed fingers and bruised knuckles from over-eager players, the rule was changed allowing them to *drop* the puck between their sticks.

Ice hockey has played a big role in modern Olympic history. The game has been a part of the Winter Games since 1920, with Canadian and Russian teams capturing the biggest share of Gold Medals.

HOCKEY QUIZ

Hockey players seldom say right out in so many words exactly what they mean. For instance, here are three hockey terms that all mean the same thing: *upstairs, top shelf,* and *toy department.* Can you explain their meaning?

17

Lacrosse

A Truly American Game — and a Fast One

You've read sports headlines that talked about "massacres" on the playing field. They meant one-sided scores, of course. But here's a sport, *lacrosse*, that has a real blood-and-guts massacre in its history. Lacrosse is one of a very few modern sports that originated in North America. (Basketball, volleyball, and ice hockey also come to mind.) Add one more distinction: lacrosse was the fastest game on foot until ice hockey outpaced it.

When pioneers began exploring Canada, they reported that the Indian tribes were playing a wild and woolly game, sometimes with as many as 500 to 1,000 braves on a side. They were using curious sticks to carry and toss a stuffed deerskin ball up and down an open field. And there seemed to be no limit to the amount of field they used. The Indians called this fast-paced mayhem *baggataway* and, though it looked like sport, they took it very seriously. Women of the opposing tribes ran along the sidelines whacking at their own players with switches and exhorting them to greater effort. The players themselves operated on the principle that the more opposing players they could cripple with the sticks they carried, the better. When both teams had thus been battered down to a manageable size, the remaining players got down to "playing the game" and concentrated on scoring.

French Canadians watching baggataway matches didn't known what to call the game, but they said the funny sticks the Indians carried reminded them of a curled bishop's crozier. So they began referring to the game as *la crosse* before they ever played it. It was some time later that the two French words were joined to make *lacrosse*.

Now, about that massacre business. It happened on June 4, 1765 at Fort Michillimackinac (now simply Mackinac) in Canada. We won't go into tribal or French versus English politics, but large delegations of Sac and Chippewa Indians were assembled at the fort to celebrate, of all things, the birthday of King George III. (He's the monarch who triggered the American Revolution.) A baggataway game was to be part of the Indian celebration, but the fort commander, suspecting something was amiss, shut the gates and declared that all soldiers and white civilians would stay inside. The Indians obliged by playing their game just outside the walls of the fort so, they said, the insiders could watch.

The game started with masses of Sacs and Chippewas surging back and forth. Indian squaws sat on the sidelines next to the fort walls. Despite the warm June day, they all were draped in blankets. As the game's excitement rose, trappers and traders inside the fort opened the gates and strolled outside for a closer look. Suddenly, on a signal from one of the chiefs, the braves rushed to the squaws

To French clerics, the lacrosse stick looked like a bishop's crosier.

who handed them tomahawks from beneath their blankets, then rushed into the fort to take the white men by surprise.

According to the most authoritative report of the massacre that followed, only three of the fort's occupants survived. The commander, Captain Etherington, and a Lieutenant Leslie were taken captive, but later released. A civilian, Alexander Henry, managed to escape and later wrote an account of the affair in a book titled, *Travels and Adventures in Canada and the Indian Territories*.

This bloody incident aside, baggataway — or lacrosse — caught the fancy of Canadian settlers, and they began trying their own versions of the game. By 1834, an exhibition match between Iroquois and Algonquin Indians was staged in the enclosure of a Montreal race course. Since the Indian game ordinarily covered more territory than a race course paddock, certain rules had to be devised for them to play in the limited space. Many believe this was the first attempt at drawing up the rules of lacrosse as the game is presently played, but the credit generally goes to a Montreal dentist, William G. Beers, who wrote a complete set of rules in 1867.

Beers had a hand in getting parliament to adopt lacrosse as Canada's national game and also arranged tours of Great Britain by a team of Caughnawaga Indians. By 1874, there were lacrosse teams in Australia, and three years later in England. It's not surprising that Dr. Beers earned the title "father of modern lacrosse."

Once lacrosse was off and running in Canada, the game quickly jumped the border into New York. In 1877, there were several clubs in that and other New England states. New York University soon had a team. Harvard and Princeton quickly followed suit. Today lacrosse is a popular sport in colleges, particularly in the eastern part of the United States.

As a sport for girls, lacrosse is also strong in the United States and Canada. But it took a decidedly long way around. When, thanks to Dr. Beers, the Canadian Indian team played exhibition games in England with Queen Victoria looking on, women spectators saw possibilities in the game for themselves. They changed the rules to emphasize speed and skill, with less brawn and body contact. Then they exported feminine lacrosse back to North America. According to this roundabout scenario, Florence Applebee, an Englishwoman who had introduced women's field hockey in America, was conducting a hockey camp in Pennsylvania. She invited Joyce Reilly to come from England as a teacher. Whereupon Ms. Reilly urged everybody at the camp to try the new lacrosse instead. In 1912, Sargent College in Boston and Sweet Briar College in Virginia became the first women's schools to adopt lacrosse.

Female lacrosse players have never been in Olympic competition, but men's teams have competed twice — in 1904 and 1908. As might be expected, Canadians won the Gold Medal both times.

Lacrosse moved into the professional ranks in the same way ice hockey went pro. But in lacrosse's case, it didn't work out. Around the turn of the century, several Ontario towns began making secret payments to outstanding players to attract winning lacrosse teams. The practice soon emerged into the open, and full-scale pro teams were playing. The pro sport faded briefly during World War I, then made a comeback following the war. For reasons unknown — probably lack of organization or perhaps mismanagement — professional lacrosse slumped once more. By 1932, it was again an amateur sport.

LACROSSE QUIZ

Compare the rules. Though lacrosse usually is played on a field 110 yards long, the game resembles another popular sport. What sport is that? Compare the footgear and equipment used in the two sports.

18

Skiing

Traveling on a Splinter Cut from a Log

As early as the Stone Age, there were men — and probably women — gliding over the snows of northern Europe and Asia on skis made of the smoothed bones of large animals. They tied them to their feet with leather thongs.

Later, some sharp thinker among them figured he could do better on strips of wood. We know that happened a long time ago because 4,000-year-old cave drawings in Norway show skiers on very long, straight skis. Also, ancient wooden skis have been found buried in the bogs of Norway and Finland. The most famous of these is the *Hoting ski*, now in a Stockholm museum and believed to be 5,000 years old. Even back then someone had sense enough to put a groove along the center of the bottom, a guiding device still used on modern skis.

Skiing was so important to the ancient Scandinavians that they worshipped a giant Goddess of Ski named *Skada* or *Skade*, as well as *Ullr* (sometimes spelled *Uller*), the God of Winter. Pictures of Uller always show him on skis. He was so big, he strapped on turned-up skis that looked like Viking ships to do his cross-country traveling.

The word *ski* also has its roots in Scandinavia. It once meant "a splinter cut from a log," but the Norsemen later changed the meaning of the word to "shoe" and pronounced it "shee." In our Anglicized language we pronounce the "k".

Being a handy way to get around in winter, skiing was also adapted for military use. The first such recorded use was in a battle in 1200 A.D. Both the Swedish and Norwegian armies were bogged down in deep snow, so King Sverre of Sweden sent scouts on skis to spy out the enemy positions. Apparently the maneuver was a great success, for by the 1500s all Swedish soldiers were equipped with skis, and the armies of other countries were following suit.

The Swedes had a nickname for their ski-clad soldiers, in the same vein that we call modern military men "GIs," "footsloggers," "leathernecks," and more. Though their skis usually were made of spruce or pine, the Swedish troopers were called *birch legs*.

Skiing as a means of everyday transportation spread to the rest of Europe about 1590, and in following centuries the much-travelling Scandinavians introduced skis just about everywhere in the world there is snow; in Australia in the 1850s, for example, and in Alaska in 1890.

It is, of course, possible that the first skis in North America were devised by Canadian Indians, who already were familiar with snowshoes. Or perhaps they copied the faster skis from early explorers and immigrants from northern Europe. In any case, ski events were included in Canadian winter carnivals as early as 1759.

Probably the first skis in the United States were brought here in the 1840s by Norwegians, as well as other Scandinavians, who settled first in New England, then moved westward. The original

"Ski" is early Scandinavian meaning "a splinter cut from a log."

ski club in the United States was established by Scandinavians at Berlin, New Hampshire in 1872.

The fact that clubs were popping up in the snow belt across the continent is proof that the skiers already were turning their skills into recreation and competition. Actually the fun part of skiing was already well under way in Europe. In 1767, Norwegian soldiers held a ski competition near Christiania (now Oslo). They had to ski down a slope without touching several bushes, thus setting the stage for what is now called the *slalom*. Some other skiing "firsts" in Norway were the world's first *ski jumping* competition in 1840 and the first *cross-country* ski races in 1866. The first international ski derby was held at Holmenkollen, Norway in 1892.

It comes as a surprise that the Swiss, with all their ready-made Alpine ski slopes at hand, weren't into skiing from the very beginning. Skiing as a recreation didn't start in the Alps until 1888, and it was an Englishman, not a Norwegian or Swede, who was responsible. That year a Colonel Napier took skis to Davos, Switzerland, and the locals thought he had lost some of his marbles when he started gliding all over the countryside. But when Sir Arthur Conan Doyle, the creator of Sherlock Holmes, joined the colonel in a cross-country tour the following year, the Swiss began to think there might be something to this crazy skiing activity after all. Today the slopes are loaded.

Meanwhile, skiing in the United States had spread all the way across the continent. Miners in the California gold rush of 1849 staged impromptu downhill races in the 1850s, thanks to the example set by a legendary mail carrier who mushed about on skis and snowshoes. He was John "Snowshoe" Thompson, a native of Norway, who toted 100-pound packs of mail from Placerville, California to Carson City, Nevada — a distance of ninety-one miles. He usually made the mountainous trip in the deepest snows in about three days, or a week for a round trip — and did it for twenty years. The miners, noting the ease with which Thompson glided along, devised skis of their own and soon were betting gold dust on the results of races straight down the mountainsides.

The first ski jumpers we know of in the United States were a couple of brothers in Red Wing, Minnesota. They, too, were of Scandinavian descent. In the 1880s, Mikkel and Torgus Hemmestvedt dazzled their friends by leaping on skis from a hill near their home. They were obviously having so much fun that their friends took to jumping, too, and the high-flying sport was on its way. Cross-country skiing for fun was also gaining fans. Perhaps the best-known cross-country skier in Canada was Herman "Jackrabbit" Smith-Johannsen. Born in Oslo in 1875, he put on his first skis when he was two years old. After immigrating to the U.S. and then to Canada, he was still skiing and teaching in the Laurentian Mountains of Quebec when he was 100 years old.

Interest in skiing as a sport increased very gradually in North America until the third Winter Olympics were held at Lake Placid, New York in 1932. The events so captivated the spectators, they determined to have a go at skiing, too. From then on the sport in the United States and Canada grew by leaps and bounds and downhill runs.

One form of downhill skiing, as you know, is the *slalom*. The word comes from two words in Norwegian (of course). *Sla* means "a little slope," and *lom* refers to the track left by something dragged in the snow.

Incidentally and for the record, in amateur and professional competition, there are fewer injuries in ski jumping than there are in downhill and slalom racing.

Sir Arthur Conan Doyle, creator of Sherlock Holmes, was an avid cross-country skier.

SKIING QUIZ

Ski competition is divided into two basic groups. Can you name them and explain what type of skiing is included in each?

19

Softball

A Time-Filler that More than Filled the Bill

Looking for a brand-new game? Get yourself a bunch of guys with time on their hands and somebody is sure to come up with a new gimmick to fill the time. Then get yourself a World's Fair to show off the game, and it will become a runaway favorite for all ages and both sexes.

That's what happened with *softball*. Back in 1895, Lewis Rober, a fireman in Minneapolis, Minnesota, started tinkering with ideas to amuse and occupy his fellow firemen while they waited around the firehouse between alarms. They all liked baseball, but couldn't play it in winter. So Rober squeezed the game of baseball down to indoor size with a smaller bat and a bigger, softer ball, which he made himself.

There's another scenario regarding the origin of softball. It tells us it happened on a gloomy afternoon in 1887, eight years before Rober's firehouse creation, and it was inside a boat club shed in Chicago. Trapped inside by rain, a fellow named George W. Hancock took a broom and started batting an old boxing glove about. From this, the story goes, Hancock and fellow club members developed the baseball-type game.

But historians score more RBIs for Rober and his fire-eaters. They liked the game he devised and took to it like a house afire. Soon other fire companies were playing it and, when the weather improved, moved their game outdoors. There it grabbed the fancy of passersby, and they, too, wanted to get in on the new game.

Fireman Lewis Rober gets the most credit for inventing softball.

Softball was on its way—at least in Minneapolis and the neighboring city of St. Paul.

Girls were playing the game right from the start. As a result, some joker writing for the sports pages dubbed it *kitten ball*, a name that stuck for some time. It has also been called *ladies' baseball, soft baseball, playground ball, indoor baseball, indoor-outdoor ball, pumpkin ball, twilight ball, diamond ball,* and *recreation baseball*. In 1933, Walter Hakanson, a physical instructor at the Denver, Colorado YMCA, coined the name *softball*. That's the one that stuck. In fact, it forced sportswriters to start calling regulation baseball *hardball* to distinguish between the two games.

By 1900, Minneapolis had the first-ever softball league, and the first rules were published in 1906. As the game spread across the continent in all directions, Canadians began playing it in 1920.

There were several reasons for softball's growing popularity. For one thing, the bats, balls, and gloves used in the game were cheaper than regulation baseball gear. An even bigger reason was the smaller area needed for a softball diamond. The game could be played in any vacant lot and most city parks.

Oddly, an economic depression is another reason for the growth of the game. With many thousands of men and women out of work and with nothing better to do, some of them spent time at recreation centers. There they saw boys and girls playing the new softball game and began playing it themselves. Meanwhile two Chicago men, sportswriter Leo H. Fischer and M.J. Pauley, saw in softball a way to relieve the boredom of those out-of-work people with nothing to do. It had worked for firemen in Minneapolis, so why not for the unemployed in Chicago?

The team of Fischer and Pauley was so successful in promoting softball games and tournaments for all ages that they even convinced officials of the 1933 World's Fair in Chicago that an exhibition softball tournament should be included in the Century of Progress events. They mustered twenty teams from across the country, and despite the different rules by which most of them had been playing, the "championship" series was an immense success — with the women's playoff drawing the biggest crowds. One notable thing the tournament accomplished was to bring softball to the attention of people from all over North America.

You know the story from there. You've probably played the game yourself and watched dozens, maybe hundreds, of other games, because softball is now played by everyone from Little Leaguers to senior citizens, both male and female. There are school, industrial, business, professional, and semi-pro softball leagues in more than thirty countries. The first "World Series" was a women's tournament in Melbourne, Australia in 1965. A men's international tournament was played the following year in Mexico City.

George Hancock devised a similar game in a Chicago boat club.

SOFTBALL QUIZ

1. We play two types of softball—*fast pitch* and *slow pitch*. Can you explain the difference between the two?

2. Regulation baseball bats may be up to forty-two inches long. How long (in inches) may a softball bat be?

3. A regulation baseball is nine to nine and a quarter inches around. What is the circumference (in inches) of a softball for fast pitch and for slow pitch?

4. Assuming there isn't a tie, how many innings are played in a regulation softball game?

Back in 1942 at Kenosha, Wisconsin, a game went for forty-two innings. The winning pitcher, Corky Corraeini, went the whole distance.

20

Tennis

Anyone for "Le Jeu de Paume"?

So you're playing tennis and your opponent is giving you a hard time. You step up to serve, deliver a smashing cannonball just over the net, and say under your breath, "Take that!"

If that ever happens to you, you can appreciate how the game of tennis got its name. It comes from a French exclamation "Tenez!", very loosely translated as "Take heed!", which French players used to shout when the ball was served.

That's only one theory about the origin of the name, however. Tennis-like games have been played for centuries all around the world. Homer, the ancient Greek poet, mentioned that Nausicaa, the daughter of King Alcinous of Phaeacia, and her handmaidens played a form of handball from which the modern game of tennis is believed to be an outgrowth. There was even an ancient version of the game using racquets. It was played at the Byzantine court and was called *tzkanion*. But it wasn't your polite sort of game that makes you think of tennis. It was played on horseback! English and French crusaders saw it and played it there. They tried to import the game into Europe when they returned, but with no success. The handball-like granddaddy of tennis with no horsing around fared much better.

Fortunately, we're not stuck with a tongue-twister like *tzkanion*, but any one of several names from ancient days might have caught on. For instance, some people theorize that tennis comes from the Greek name *phennis*, or from the word *teniludius*, the name the Romans gave to a similar game. One popular theory about the game's name is that it was adopted from the Egyptian city of Tinnis (also called Tanis) where fine linens were manufactured. Centuries ago tennis balls were covered with a light fabric resembling linen that may have come from the Nile delta city. Hence, the story goes, people played with *tinnis* balls and that's how the name of the game got started.

Wooden paddles replaced the sore palms of "jeu de paume."

In any event, the game — or games similar to it — was very popular in countries on both sides of the Mediterranean Sea. From there it spread all over Europe. In France in particular the game was a runaway favorite with royalty and, of course, with the social-climbers who hoped the aristocrats would drop in for tea and crumpets and perhaps a couple of sets on the tennis court.

At this time the game was still played by batting the ball back and forth with the palm of the hand. So the French quite literally called it *Le Jeu de Paume*. If the game was played out-of-doors, they called it *Le Jeu de Longue Paume*, and when indoor courts were built, they referred to the game as *Le Jeu de Courte Paume*. The French talk a very good game of tennis.

The French royalty favored indoor courts and had a lot of them. But the first private indoor tennis court was built in Poitiers in the year 1230 by a *gentilhomme* named Peter Garnier. A Phillipe le Bel built a dandy one in Paris in 1308, and Benvenuto Cellini, the noted Florentine sculptor, wrote home in 1540 to say he had played a game or two there. Cellini was attached to the royal court of Francis I at the time.

Even the French monks became tennis freaks, playing the game in their cloisters and courtyards. They became so preoccupied with the game that the Archbishop of Rouen banned it — for the monks, at least — in 1245.

Meanwhile, back at the palace the king, counts, dukes, and duchesses were happily building ornate indoor playing areas and yelling "Tenez!" at each other as a royal pastime. The paved floor was marked off in a manner similar to modern tennis courts and a loose-hanging net was draped across the center. The ball was bounced off thirty-foot-high walls as it was volleyed back and forth.

As late as 1632, when a book of rules was published, the players were still not using racquets to hit the ball. But the game probably required as much fast footwork and heated exercise as modern tennis. In fact, still another theory about the origin of the name of the game is that it comes from an Arabic word, *tanaz*, meaning "to leap or to bound." In 1316, King Louis X is said to have died of a chill he caught drinking beakers of cold water after a vigorous and sweaty game of palm bashing.

At some point in the game's development, tennis buffs must have gotten tired of having sore palms. Wooden paddles appeared for batting the ball. Then came ponderous netted *raquettes*, forerunners of what we use today.

This development made le jeu de paume a misleading name. But English royalty, who had also become hooked on the game, took care of that. They also picked up the French shout, "Tenez!" Of course, they mispronounced it, and thus we got the name *tennis*. Ironically, the mangled French word was backhanded across the English Channel and today the French also call the game *tennis*.

Early on the English abandoned the handball kind of tennis. In fact, the first reference to the game in English literature is in Geoffrey Chaucer's *Troilus and Criseyde*, written in 1385, in which he said: "But canstow playen racket to and fro." Chaucer wouldn't get far as a sportswriter today.

Half a century later Henry VIII, that fellow who kept switching wives, at least knew what he liked for recreation. He was a full-scale tennis buff and had indoor courts built at Whitehall, St. James Palace, and Hampton Court Palace. The one at Hampton Court is the oldest tennis court in England and it's still in use.

How did we get the term *tennis court*? A logical assumption, and probably true, is that the term comes from the fact that the game was originally played principally by French courtiers and members of the English royal court. Thus they called the game *court tennis*, and began referring to the indoor playing areas as *tennis courts*. When the game was moved outdoors onto grassy areas, it became known as *lawn tennis*.

The method of scoring tennis — 15, 30, 40, and game — also goes back to ancient times. It was picked up from an old Italian ball game called *pallone*, which in turn was descended from earlier games played by the Romans, who got them from the Greeks, who copied them from the Arabs and points east. Two French words also are sources of terms used in modern scoring, thanks to our habit of mispronouncing anything that comes out of France. A tie in the game when each side scores 40 is called a *deuce*, a garbling of the French word for "two." The word *love*, meaning no score, is a corruption of the French term "l'oeuf," meaning the big fat zero that we call a goose egg or zilch. End up with a "love" score in tennis and you've got egg on your face.

There are a couple of other notions about how "love" got into tennis scoring instead of "nothing." Since the early English tennis buffs were avid gamblers, one theory says the term "love" comes from the expression "to play for money or play for love." In other words, for money or nothing. The other idea gives the expression "labour of love," or doing something for nothing, as the source. You can take your pick.

When the ball is served and strikes the net in tennis, perhaps you've heard someone call it a *let ball* instead of the more common *net ball*. Both are correct. The term "let ball" comes from the Old English word, *letten* or *laeten*, which means "to hinder." Thus a served ball that was hindered by the net was called a let ball. Net ball came into use later on.

Though it is said to be one of the quietest and politest of sports (that was in pre-McEnroe days), tennis in the time of its early popularity in France was one of the noisiest. Players shrieked at one another across the net, and spectators bellowed from the galleries. So much cursing was included in the uproar that a set of rules issued at the end of the sixteenth century warned the players to cut out the swearing and blasphemy. In tournament play, a fine of five "sols" was levied for every oath. A dirty-mouthed player could win a game and lose a bundle in the process. Nevertheless, some saw a benefit in all the shouting and jeering. In 1780, the surgeon general of the French army maintained that the game of tennis (when played at its vocal best) had a healthy effect on the throat and lungs.

Tennis almost died out during the French Revolution as many of the players and fans lost their royal heads. Across the channel, the English civil war against Charles I, who also lost his head, had the same discouraging effect on the sport. But enthusiasm gradually revived, especially after the game was moved out-of-doors onto grass. There it picked up the name *lawn tennis*. Though it is now played both indoors and out, the accepted name is *lawn tennis*, a term adopted officially in the 1850s to distinguish it from the earlier name, *court tennis*.

A Welshman, Major Walter Clopton Wingfield, is given a large measure of credit for adapting the game to its present form. He laid out a court without walls on the lawn of his home in Wales and introduced his version of tennis at a garden party in 1873. It gained immediate popularity. Trouble was, the major called his game *Sphairistike*, a Greek word meaning "playing ball." The tongue-twister name never caught on.

The spread of modern tennis around the world is partly due to its introduction in various countries by the British military forces. The game came to the United States in 1874 from Bermuda with the aid of an enterprising young woman who was vacationing there. Mary Outerbridge, of Staten Island, New York, played tennis with British officers in Bermuda and liked the game so much she brought a net and several racquets and balls with her when she returned home. There was a hassle at the New York docks because the customs inspectors had never seen the sports gear before and didn't know its purpose or value. They held it for a time while they pondered the matter, then finally released it duty-free.

Miss Outerbridge had some difficulty talking her baseball-playing brothers into trying the new game. They thought anything using terms like "love" was a sissy sport and best left to the girls. But their sister was persuasive, pointing out that army officers played tennis, which required speed and skill. The result: the boys were won over. Thus encouraged, Miss Outerbridge talked the Staten Island Cricket and Baseball Club into trying the game, and in the spring of 1874 they set up what is believed to be the first tennis court in North America. A close runner-up would be a court laid out in the same year by Dr. James Dwight on the William Appleton estate at Nahant, Massachusetts, near Boston. Doctor Dwight, often called "the father of American tennis," was a dedicated tennis pioneer who did much to introduce and promote the now-popular game in the United States and Canada. With Richard Sears, he won the U.S. doubles championship five times.

The first national tennis championship in this country was played in 1881 at Newport, Rhode Island. Richard Sears won the singles crown, and W.E. Glyn was the runner-up. Clarence M. Clark and F.W. Taylor won the doubles competition.

The first national women's title matches were held six years later at the Philadelphia Cricket Club. Ellen F. Hansell was the winner. Women's doubles were started at Philadelphia in 1890. The winners were two sisters, Grace W. and Ellen C. Roosevelt.

Beginning in 1960, Margaret Smith Court of Australia is said to have won more major tennis titles than any other person, male or female, in the history of the sport. Another kind of record, one that stood for more than seventy years, was set around the turn of the century at Wimbledon, England, a mecca for all tennis buffs. In a match between a Mrs. Satterwaithe and a Mrs. Lamber-Chambers, the ball was volleyed back and forth across the net ninety times during a rally for a single crucial point.

While we're speaking of the ladies, here's a fashion note. When Maud Watson won England's first Ladies' Singles Championship in 1884, she was dressed in an ankle-length dress with a billowing skirt, long sleeves, and a high neckline. The full-length skirts lasted until 1919 because any young lady, even a tennis player, who exposed her ankles in public was considered a brazen hussy.

Over the years, however, daring females who wanted more freedom of movement on the court began to appear in increasingly higher hemlines, thoroughly shocking the spectators each time more calf or a knee was exposed. They also began to play in short sleeves and lower, more comfortable necklines. It wasn't until 1933 that America's Helen Jacobs became the first world-class female player who dared appear at a major tennis match in shorts!

Naturally, every sport has to have a cup, the coveted top prize. In tennis it's the Davis Cup, first put up in 1900 by Dwight F. Davis when he was still an undergraduate at Harvard. Davis was three times national doubles champion. He later became a lawyer and served as Assistant Secretary of War in President Coolidge's cabinet. President Hoover appointed him Governor General of the Philippines in 1929.

The Davis Cup is really a large silver bowl, and its official title is the "International Lawn Tennis Challenge Trophy." It was originally intended for competition between the United States and Great Britain, including Canada. (Davis was on the winning team at the first two tourneys.) In 1904, Belgium and France joined the competition, and it was later opened to tennis players all over the world.

"Tenez" was just another way of saying "Take that!"

TENNIS QUIZ

Get out your measuring tape and answer these questions about the dimensions of a regulation lawn tennis court.

1. What are the length and width of the court for singles play?

2. What are the length and width of the court for doubles play?

3. A 4½ foot strip along each side of the court provides the additional area for doubles play. What is the strip called?

4. How high is the net at the center of the court?

5. How high is the net where it is attached to the side posts?

6. How far is the service line from the net?

21

Table Tennis

Plenty of "Inventors," More than Enough Names

Gotta coin? You'll need to flip it to decide who originated the capsule version of tennis known as *table tennis*. There are a number of claimants to the honor — almost as many as there are names for the game. Even the game's popularity has had as many ups and downs as a Ping-Pong™ ball.

As for the "inventor" of table tennis, it depends on which sport historian you believe. They give the credit to: a) a British army officer in South Africa in the 1870s; b) a British army officer in India in the 1860s or thereabouts; c) "somebody" in England in the nineteenth century. There is even a claim that table tennis was invented by a New England Yankee in the 1890s. But the rug is pulled from under that claim by an advertisement for table tennis equipment that appeared in a London newspaper ten years earlier.

What we do know about the origins of table tennis is that at first the game was played with just about any kind of equipment that came to hand. The "net" often was a line of books up-ended on a table. The paddles were simply stiff pieces of cardboard, and balls were made of tightly-wrapped string, cork, or rubber. Moms must have had something to say about the game because the solid balls were covered with woven netting to keep them from scratching the furniture.

Perhaps the biggest credit for improving the game and standardizing equipment should go to Parker Bros. of Salem, Massachusetts, manufacturers of games, and to Hamley Bros., London, the Parker company's agents. Between them they were responsible for most of the "new, improved" developments in table tennis. For example, in addition to miniature nets, they also introduced racquets that were small copies of tennis racquets, then switched to wooden paddles. These were called *battledores* because they looked like the wooden paddles of that name that were used to pound laundry in Victorian times. Shorten battledore and you get *bat*, a term often used for table tennis paddles today.

Experts at the game experimented with various surfaces like vellum and sandpaper on the paddles to get better control of the ball. But credit goes to a Mr. Good of London (his full name isn't known) for introducing in 1902 the studded rubber surface so popular among modern table tennis buffs.

There are two stories about how the celluloid "ping-pong" ball came to the game. One says an Englishman named James Gibb

Be thankful it's not still called "Whiff Whaff" or "Flim Flam."

visited America and, while watching children play table tennis with solid cork and rubber balls, got the idea that hollow celluloid balls would be better. The other story simply says that around the turn of the century an unidentified Englishman — some say a clergyman — walked into Hamley Bros. with some celluloid balls and they took it from there.

As might be expected, several game manufacturers in addition to the Parkers and Hamleys saw the profit potentials in the game and began promoting it — and their equipment — under names such as *indoor tennis, miniature indoor lawn tennis, Gossima, Flim Flam,* and *Whiff Whaff.* The Hamleys were first to name the game Ping-Pong™, because, they said, "ping" was the sound made when the bat hit the ball and "pong" was heard when the ball hit the table. So now you know.

Light and portable, it's little wonder that table tennis spread around the world in the latter part of the nineteenth century. For a short time it was the "in" game of English aristocrats, but the general public soon took it over and mammoth tournaments were held all over Europe. In no time at all other countries, particularly Czechoslovakia, were producing the table tennis champions.

Then, for reasons no one can explain, the table tennis craze lost its popularity. It was revived briefly in 1902 when Mr. Good's improved paddle offered better control of the ball, then waned again. A second revival came in the 1920s when Parker Bros. in the United States and Hamley Bros. in England reintroduced the game under the name Ping-Pong™. In 1923, a Ping-Pong Association was formed in England. But when they were informed that Ping-Pong was a copyrighted trade name, the name was changed to the English Table Tennis Association. An International Table Tennis Federation was formed in 1916 — and "table tennis" has been the name of the game ever since.

As competition and interest increased around the world, it was natural that table tennis should have a championship cup like tennis's Davis Cup and hockey's Stanley Cup. The one for table tennis is called the *Swaythling Cup* and it first appeared at Oxford University in the 1920s. Ivor Montagu, an Oxford student and a dyed-in-the-wool table tennis freak, persuaded his mother, Lady Swaythling, to donate a cup to be awarded to the winners of the annual Oxford-Cambridge table tennis matches. The Swaythling Cup has since become an international trophy and is to table tennis what the Davis Cup is to big brother tennis.

By the way, don't confuse *paddle tennis* with table tennis. The paddle game was devised at the beginning of this century by the

Reverend Frank P. Beal, then secretary of the Community Council of New York. He was a tennis enthusiast and wanted something similar for kids to play because he thought they couldn't handle the regulation tennis racquets or lob the ball the full length of the court.

The Reverend Beal simply cut the court dimensions in half, lowered the net to thirty inches, and substituted paddles for tennis racquets. The game became so popular with youngsters all over the country that adults developed their own versions, including *platform paddle tennis* and *paddle ball*. The latter is similar to handball, but a paddle is used instead of swatting the ball with a gloved hand.

Some called it "Battledore" because the bats looked like those the laundresses used.

TABLE TENNIS QUIZ

Unlike any other competitive sport, table tennis has a rule regarding the color of clothing worn in matches. Do you know what it is?

22

Track and Field

Forgotten for Centuries, Now Star of the Olympic Games

A prehistoric caveman is wandering through the jungle looking for lunch. Suddenly a sabre-tooth tiger appears. Right then and there man learned to jump and run. Maybe he paused long enough to heave a rock or stick — and learned two more things that we go to watch at the Olympic Games today.

In other words, *track and field* events, the star attractions of the Olympics and other international games, are a direct result of primitive man's survival skills. If he didn't run fast enough or heave a rock well enough, *he* was the lunch, not the tiger.

Thus, it's not surprising that many of the athletic contests now included in track and field programs can be traced back to the misty days before recorded history. There is even a legend in Ireland about the *Tailtin Games* held in County Meath in 1829 B.C. It's a cinch they weren't playing tiddlywinks.

Before we go on talking about *athletes* and *athletics*, let's take a look at the meaning of the words. No matter how good you are at running, jumping, throwing, and other physical skills, you aren't truly an athlete until you've been in a competition. The word comes from a mouthful of Greek words like *athlos*, meaning "a contest," *athlon*, the "prize," and *athletes*, meaning "a competitor." To the Greeks, *athletics* included politics, mathematics, and anything else in which people matched skills. In the strict sense of the word, then, a chess player was an athlete. Not to worry, these days we only associate athletes with muscles.

Prehistoric man learned to take hurdles at an early age.

Some athletic skills were already hoary with age when the first Olympic race was run in 776 B.C. The same is true today. A Greek athlete running or throwing a javelin in the ancient Olympics would be right at home at a twentieth century Olympiad. However, he'd have scant chance of winning a medal. Modern athletes are better trained and in better physical shape than the ancients were. World speed and distance records are broken year after year.

We know the Romans took over the Olympic Games when they conquered the Greeks, and that Emperor Theodosius discontinued the games in 393 A.D. But nobody knows why running, jumping, and throwing contests didn't go on in Europe despite the emperor's disapproval. Maybe it was just too tough to make a living, especially in the Dark Ages. Anyway, there was no mention of athletics in history for the next eight or nine centuries.

But you can't keep a good thing down. By the twelfth century, track and field events were back in full swing. The revival probably first occurred in England. As early as 1154, open fields were set aside in London for the practice and enjoyment of running, jumping, and weight throwing.

All went well for the athletes for 200 years, then King Edward III clamped down on the track and field activities, as well as most other sports, for a reason that has been mentioned in previous chapters about football and golf. The king didn't want young men wasting time in "unprofitable" sports when they should be practicing with longbows for defense of the country. Several other monarches banned various forms of athletics for the same reason, and it wasn't until armies were using muskets and cannon that the bans were lifted. They had often been ignored anyway, and by 1414 sports, including track and field, were again given the royal nod and public participation.

English colleges and universities took up track and field, too. In 1864, Oxford and Cambridge held the first intercollegiate meet on record. Meanwhile, in the United States there was an athletic club in San Francisco in 1860, but the first known track and field meet in this country was held by the New York Athletic Club in 1868. It was an indoor event. American universities and colleges soon were competing in track and field meets, and the stage was set for entry into the Olympics when the Games were revived in Athens in 1896. United States athletes won nine of the twelve track and field events at those Games.

Track and Field competition, as the name implies, is divided into two groups of events. The track events include: *sprints* (or *dashes*) of up to 220 yards, *longer races, relays, hurdles, steeplechases* involving hurdles and water jumps, *cross-country races, marathons,* and *walking*. Field events include: *broad jump, high jump, triple jump* (hop, step, jump), *pole vault, shot-put, discus throw, javelin throw, hammer throw,* and *weight throw*. There are also a *decathlon* for men, which combines ten events over two days, and a *heptathlon* for women including seven events.

You're not an "athlete" unless you are in competition.

TRACK AND FIELD QUIZ

For many scores of years track runners aspired to run a mile in four minutes. Who finally cracked the four-minute-mile barrier, and when?

23

Volleyball

A Truly Amateur Sport, and Fun for the Whole Family

Imagine it's the year 1895 and a cluster of portly businessmen is standing in the YMCA gymnasium in Holyoke, Massachusetts. They're dressed in gym clothes and ready for a weekly workout under the supervision of William G. Morgan, the Y director.

"Gentlemen," says Morgan, "today we're going to try a new game I've dreamed up. There's not as much body contact as in the basketball you've been playing. So stop beefing about your bruises."

"How does it go?"

"See that tennis net I've strung up across the gym? The top of it is seven feet off the floor. You're going to divide up into two teams and bat this rubber basketball bladder back and forth across the net with your hands. The team that knocks the bladder out of bounds or fails to get it across the net gives a point to the other side."

"Sounds good, Morgan. What's the name of the game?"

"I call it *minonette*."

"Minonette! Sheesh! Sounds sissy."

"Don't you believe it. This new game isn't as strenuous as basketball, but you'll work up a sweat for sure. Okay, gents, let's play."

"Minonette. You sure this isn't a girls' game, Morgan?"

Needless to say, if you recognize the game Morgan described, it became a worldwide favorite in a comparatively short time. Also needless to say, Morgan's friends talked him out of the name "minonette" and suggested *volleyball* instead. The ball, they pointed out, is "volleyed" back and forth, a word from the French *vol*, meaning "flying."

Actually, Morgan can't be said to be the first person with the volleyball idea. It is somewhat similar to an Italian game played in the Middle Ages. From Italy, it migrated to Germany where it was called *faustball*. (*Faust* means "fist" in German.) Morgan's chief innovation was the rule that the ball may not touch the floor.

He also experimented with various heights for the net and a better, smaller ball. Today, the top of a regulation volleyball net is eight feet from the floor at the center. The measure is seven and a half feet for women's play. The inflated, leather-covered volleyball is between twenty-six and twenty-seven inches around, slightly smaller than a basketball. The court size is thirty feet wide and sixty feet long.

Fitness buffs tried "Minonette" at the Holyoke, Massachusetts YMCA.

A year after he introduced the game, Morgan presented his handwritten rules for volleyball at a meeting of YMCA physical directors at Springfield College in Massachusetts, the place where basketball was invented four years earlier. Since then, the rules, court size, and six players per side have remained fairly stable, except in the Orient where nine players often make up a side and play is on a larger court with a lower net.

From the 1896 meeting at Springfield College, YMCA missionaries took the indoor/outdoor game of volleyball around the world. American soldiers helped spread the game overseas in both world wars. More than thirty countries now enter teams in international volleyball competitions. There are presently some efforts to organize and support professional leagues, but volleyball remains, as always, essentially an amateur sport.

Perhaps the most outstanding volleyball team ever was a girls' team in Japan called the *Nichibo team*. They scored more than 150 straight wins against women's teams around the world, then won a Gold Medal at the 1964 Olympics in Tokyo, when both men's and women's volleyball were introduced in the Games.

VOLLEYBALL QUIZ

Considered an excellent body conditioner by physical education directors, volleyball is also said to be the best game available for correcting *student stoop*. Can you explain why?

Volleyball is played by both sexes and almost anywhere.

24

Wrestling

Grunting and Groaning Since the Beginning of Time

There is little doubt that wrestling is older than civilization. It can be traced back through the Romans and Greeks to the Middle East and ancient India. Wall paintings in Egypt show that wrestling was practiced there as "recently" as 5,000 years ago. An equally old bronze figurine found in a temple near Baghdad, Iraq shows two grapplers hard at it.

Other discoveries indicate the ancients knew just about every wrestling twist, turn, and hold used today. Maybe that's why the Anglo-Saxons dubbed the sport *wrestling* after their word *wrest*, which meant "to turn." (It's also the source of our word *wrist*.)

When he wrote the *Iliad*, Homer did wrestling's first great bit of sports reporting in Book XXIII, when he told of a match between Odysseus and mighty Ajax during the Trojan War. Achilles had been killed, so the fighting was stopped for seventeen days of mourning and "funeral games." Odysseus and Ajax wrestled, with Achilles's armor as the prize. When Odysseus beat him, Ajax took his own life in shame.

Along with discus throwers, the Greeks honored wrestlers as the finest examples of athletes. They had a freestyle, catch-as-catch-can way of wrestling that permitted strangleholds, eye gouging, breaking of fingers, biting, punching, and more. As if that weren't enough to please the fans, the Greeks introduced *pancratium*, also called *pancration*. It's from Greek words meaning "all strength," and the style of combat really took all the strength a contestant could muster. Pancratium was a combination of wrestling and boxing with no holds barred. There weren't any rest periods and the contestants fought to the finish — often death. Only when one raised his hand in defeat or lay unconscious was a match ended.

The Greeks later toned down this brutal method of fighting, but when the Romans conquered Greece they revived the bloodiest features for a time. Then they, too, dropped that mode of fighting and blended some of the Greek wrestling techniques with their own and developed what is now known as the *Greco-Roman* style of wrestling. Holds below the waist are not allowed.

Homer reported a wrestling match between Odysseus and Ajax during a lull in the Trojan War. Odysseus won.

Though wrestling was not there at the start of the original Olympic Games in Greece, the sport was included sixty-eight years later and has been in the Games, including the modern ones, ever since. Many sports may have had their ups and downs, but wrestling never entirely faded away when other athletic contests were practically zilch.

What kept the grapplers going in the Middle Ages was the desire of monarchs to maintain unbeatable armies and, if they couldn't do that, to have a stable of wrestlers to clobber the opposition. There were wrestling matches on the program at festivals, holiday revels, and royal birthdays. Wrestlers in other kingdoms often were challenged to come and compete.

This royal rivalry resulted in one oft-told tale regarding Francis I, King of France, and Henry VIII of England. There are two versions of the story. One says Francis I accepted a personal challenge from Henry VIII and managed to pin the boastful Henry to the mat. The other story says that, as Francis and Henry watched matches between wrestlers from their two countries, the English-men were getting the best of it. Henry's bragging about English superiority so enraged the hot-tempered Francis that he jumped up and grappled with his guest in an attempt to throttle him. The match was a draw, because courtiers pulled the two kings apart before any imperial damage was done.

Over the years, just about every country of the world has developed its own preferred style of wrestling. There is the *glima* style of Iceland, the *schweitzer schwingen* in Switzerland, and the *Cumberland*, a particularly savage style developed in Ireland. The Japanese are noted for their *sumo* style begun in 23 B.C. with 300- to 400-pound wrestlers. They also developed ju-*jitsu* and *judo*, which are used more for self-defense than for competition. Some countries even have regional variations. In England, for example, there are *Cornish*, *Devonshire*, and *Lancashire* styles of wrestling. The last is the roughest of all and is much favored by Scottish grapplers. The French preference is for a Greco-Roman style of wrestling, with no holds below the waist and no tripping permit-ted.

When the first European settlers arrived in North America, they found the native Indians already adept at wrestling. At first the Americans favored the Greco-Roman style for themselves, but later they switched to the freestyle wrestling now in vogue. There are certain refinements, of course. Punching, strangleholds, eye gouging, kneeing, finger breaking, hair pulling, and the like are no-no's.

A Cleveland, Ohio steel mill worker named Tom Jenkins was one of the first wrestling professionals to make a name for himself as a freestyle champ in the United States. But in 1905 he was finally pinned to the mat by Frank Gotch, who dominated American professional wrestling for the next eight years. Gotch won 154 of his 160 matches.

Since the end of World War II, professional wrestling has been more showmanship than sport. Though millions of spectators attend wrestling every year, and millions more watch on television, the outcome of the matches is almost always decided in advance. The greatest skill the "wrestlers" have is in making their acrobatics look strenuous without hurting each other. To add to the glitzy costumed show, there also are women wrestlers, midget wrestlers, tag team matches, and mud wrestling. Honest pro athletes like Jenkins and Gotch would have cried foul!

On the other hand, amateur wrestling in the United States and Canada has remained a pure sport. Athletic clubs, YMCAs, colleges, high schools, and even elementary schools have kept the sport alive and grappling through continued competition. As in boxing, the contests are divided into weight classes, and for many years all were freestyle matches. In 1953, however, a Greco-Roman championship meet was held by the Amateur Athletic Union in Toledo, Ohio, and that style of wrestling is now also seen throughout the country.

WRESTLING QUIZ

Professional wrestlers usually put on their shows in ordinary boxing rings, which actually are squares. The wrestling area used in the amateur sport is different. Can you explain this difference and tell the size of the amateur wrestling mat?

25

Other Sports

BADMINTON

This game, which is a combination of two others, got its name from Badminton, the country estate of the Duke of Beaufort in Gloucestershire, England. The game was introduced there in about 1873 by British army officers who had returned from India. It was so new it didn't have a name, so everyone simply referred to it as "the game at Badminton." Eventually, it was just called *badminton*.

If you've played or watched badminton, you know it looks a lot like tennis, except that the top of the net is five feet off the ground and a bird-like shuttlecock is used instead of a ball. Actually, it's a combination of *poona*, a game played in India, and an English children's game called *battledore and shuttlecock*. In the first, the Indians batted a parchment ball back and forth across a net with racquets. There was no net in the children's game, but they used wooden paddles (battledores) to keep a shuttlecock (the bird) in the air. The British officers, seeking recreation, simply put features of the two games together.

Badminton caught on quickly among landed gentry in the British Isles, and was imported into Canada in 1890. Shortly afterward the badminton bird was batted across the border into the United States.

BOBSLEDDING

The girls must have said, "Come on, guys, make up your minds," when bobsledding was first getting under way. The first *bobsleighs*, as they were called, carried five persons and were introduced at St. Moritz, Switzerland by vacationers who wanted something faster than the toboggans they were accustomed to. The first actual races were held in 1898 and one of the rules said that each five-person sled crew must include two females.

This was okay with both the guys and the gals until it was discovered that more weight meant more speed. So the girls (who refused to get fat?) were replaced on the sleds by bigger, heftier men. Today the girls have their own *bobsleds*. "So there!"

Two-man and four-man bobsleds now compete in the Olympic Winter Games. No girls allowed.

CANOEING

Canoes have been used in most parts of the world since primitive times. But the first use of these light craft for sport and recreation can be attributed to a British lawyer, John Macgregor, who developed a light canoe for his own pleasure in 1865. Macgregor wrote several books about canoeing throughout Scandinavia, Europe, and the Holy Land.

Canoe comes from a Haitian word, *canoa*, meaning a boat hollowed out of a log or "dugout." The word was taken to Europe by Spanish explorers, possibly even by Christopher Columbus, too.

CRICKET

The name for *cricket* comes from an Anglo-Saxon word meaning "crooked stick," the type of bat used when the game was born. Hang on to that thought, because there's another story going around that says the French invented cricket by altering the game of croquet. They called the new game *criquet*, which actually means "cricket" or "locust," so they wouldn't confuse it with *croquet*. That's hard to believe, since cricket was being played in England in the twelfth century, almost 100 years before the French ever heard of croquet.

So the Anglo-Saxon cricket is the name of the game. But even criquet would be better than the name the English called the game around 1477. For a short time, fortunately a very short time, the name of the game was *hands in and hands out*. We know of that mouthful because that's what King Edward IV called cricket when he banned it because it interfered with compulsory archery practice. A bloke could get two years in prison if caught playing cricket. The person who permitted the game to be played on his property got three years in the slammer.

Nevertheless, cricket just couldn't be put down. It made a comeback, along with other sports. In 1620, Oliver Cromwell, Lord Protector of the Commonwealth, was criticized because he played "the disreputable game of cricket." (He played football, too.) Not to worry. In 1748, the Court of the King's Bench finally declared cricket a legal sport in England.

Meanwhile, cricket hopped about the world wherever the British Empire had a colony or outpost. It came to America in about 1747, some years before the Revolution. But in the nineteenth century it was more or less abandoned in favor of the faster game of baseball. Harry Wright, manager of the Cincinnati Red Stockings, the first professional baseball team in the United States, was a former pro cricket player.

As a matter of fact, the writers of baseball rules picked up several cricket terms — such as *bat, batter, fair ball, runs, outs,* and *umpire*.

Cricket, too, has its coveted prize for winning an international championship. It's called *The Ashes*. In 1882, an Australian cricket team bewildered the English by beating them on English soil.The next day the *Sporting Times* of London published the following notice:

> "In affectionate remembrance of English Cricket which died at the Oval on the 29th of August, 1882. Deeply lamented by a large circle of sorrowing friends and acquaintances. R.I.P. The body will be cremated and the ashes taken to Australia."

When the English cricketers went to Australia the following year, they were exhorted in the press to "bring back the ashes." As a gag, women in Melbourne presented them with a five-inch-high earthenware urn filled with ashes. It is still preserved in England and serves as the symbol of an international cricket rivalry.

FIELD HOCKEY

Since *field hockey* is usually played on grassy fields, it was called just plain *hockey* until *ice hockey* came along. Then a better label was needed to tell the two apart.

Historians say a form of field hockey originated in Persia (now Iran) as far back as 2000 B.C. From there it spread east and is now the national game of India, along with cricket. It spread west, too, and was played by the Greeks before the Christian era. After a lull of some centuries, the game was revived and slowly moved across Europe. The French called it *hoquet*, a word they used for a "shepherd's crook," which resembled the curved hockey stick. It also means "hiccups."

The English developed their own version of the game, taking some features of the Irish *hurling*. They also misspelled hoquet, of course, and came up with the Anglicized *hockey*. (See Chapter 16 on ice hockey.)

Here's a switch. Field hockey was considered too rough for women until 1877. That year women's teams were formed in England and were so successful that women almost took over the game in the Western Hemisphere. Constance Applebee of the British College of Physical Education introduced field hockey in the United States while she was attending a summer course at Harvard. Harriet Ballintine, director of physical education at Vassar College, then asked Ms. Applebee to teach field hockey at her school. This she did, as well as at Wellesley, Smith, Mount Holyoke, and Bryn Mawr.

Though field hockey was all the rage among men in several other countries, American males were lukewarm to it until 1926. Then another Englishwoman, Louise Roberts, who was coaching at Rosemary Hall School for Girls in Greenwich, Connecticut, was asked to teach the game to groups of men in New York City and Westchester County. Today, thanks to the lady teacher, United States men's field hockey teams compete in the Olympic Games. The sport has been included in the Olympics since 1908, but only for males. Another switch.

HORSESHOE PITCHING

The ancient Parthian horsemen in Asia are said to be the first to put iron shoes on horses to protect their hooves. The Roman legions, who fought the Parthians, copied the practice, and soon after legionnaires (the Roman GI's) were pitching horseshoes for fun and side bets. Roman officers already were playing the game of *quoits*. But the ordinary soldiers couldn't afford the round metal discs and equipment used by the brass, so they "borrowed" horseshoes from the quartermaster. Needing targets for their pitching, they settled on wooden stakes.

The Roman legions took horseshoe pitching and quoits to Britain when they invaded in 43 A.D. From there, settlers and soldiers brought both games to North America in later centuries.

ICE BOATING

The Dutch are believed to have invented this fast and frigid sport, though people in countries around the Baltic Sea may have been ice boating at the same time. Talk about hedging your bet. The Dutch simply fastened a strong cross bar with runners under the bow of a sailboat and put an iron shoe on the rudder. No fear of thin ice; they were always afloat and dry.

Dutch immigrants brought ice boating to North America. A drawing of an ice boat first appeared in a New York publication in 1790, and that same year a man named Oliver Booth was reported ice boating on the frozen Hudson River at the town of Poughkeepsie.

Ice boating clubs, formed after the Civil War, perfected the design and began calling their speedy vehicles *ice yachts*. Around the turn of the century, one fellow was declared champion five years in a row. What makes his feat special is his name—Jack Frost.

JAI-ALAI

When Hernando Cortez, the Spanish explorer, prowled around Mexico in 1519, he reported that the Aztecs were playing a game similar to what we know today as jai-*alai* (pronounced hi-li). That may be true. But others say the game originated in the Basque region of Spain when a flat wooden bat was introduced into a handball game. Then a short basket was substituted for the bat. And finally the long curved wicker *cesta* was developed.

In several Spanish-speaking countries the game was called *pelota*, which means "ball." But the Cubans, who brought the game to the United States, preferred the Basque name *jai-alai*, meaning "merry festival." The game was introduced at the St. Louis World's Fair in 1904.

The jai-alai ball, which is about two-thirds the size of a baseball, is said to travel faster than any other ball in sports. It has been clocked at 150 miles-per-hour. Compare that with Bobby Hull's 118.3 miles-per-hour slap shot mentioned in Chapter 16 and with a pitch by baseball's Nolan Ryan. In 1974, his fastball was clocked at 100.9 mph.

JU-JITSU, JUDO, AND KARATE

Both China and Japan claim credit for the origin of *ju-jitsu*, a form of unarmed combat and self-defense. But it has been notable in the development of Japan and was first written of there in the eighth century.

However, when the time came that ju-jitsu was being considered as a possible sport, some of its techniques were considered too dangerous. So in 1882, Jigoro Kano, a ju-jitsu master, revised the ancient methods so that non-lethal competition could be staged. He called the new system *judo*, a Japanese word meaning "gentle way." Jigoro's school, the Kodokan Institute of Judo, is still operating in Tokyo on its original site.

Karate, another method of combat and self-defense, is believed to have originated in India. Statues there as old as 1000 B.C. show temple guards in karate poses. Legends also tell of warriors and priests in India who were masters of a fighting art called *vajrammushsti*. Several Buddhist writings explain the techniques. Bodhidharma, the founder of Zen Buddhism, is said to have carried the unarmed fighting method to China. There it was combined with the native *chuan-fa* method and developed into several styles of combat, which we now refer to as *kung-fu*. From China, unarmed combat and self-defense spread to Okinawa and the rest of the Orient. It is now practiced around the world.

Karate today is a remodeled form of the Chinese *kenpo* way of fighting with the hands, arms, legs, feet, and some other parts of the body. The modern name, *karate*, is Japanese, meaning "open hand," and didn't come into use until 1923.

POLO

Persia, Tibet, China, Japan, India. Take your pick and you'll find a sports historian who says the game of polo originated there. One wag describes it as "field hockey with saddle sores," but the modern game of polo took shape in about 1862 when British army officers observed the game in Punjab, India and changed certain features of it for their own use, including goal posts and a pre-scribed playing field. When they asked the Punjabis the name of the game, they were told it was called *pulu* after the "willow root" from which the ball was made. The British changed that too — to *polo*.

Members of the 10th Hussars took polo back to England with them in 1869. There it became a great favorite with those who had the cash to maintain a string of polo "ponies." A rich man's game, polo was brought to New York in 1876 by James Gordon Bennett, an American multi-millionaire. For the first few years it was played indoors.

RACQUETS AND SQUASH RACQUETS _____

If you've read Charles Dickens's *Pickwick Papers*, you may remember him mentioning the game of *racquets* as it was played by prisoners in London's debtors' prisons. The date of the origin of the game is not certain, but prisoners in the lock-up for debt were given more freedom than hardened criminals. Hence, they had the daily opportunity to go into a courtyard and bat a ball against one wall.

This game, now known simply as racquets, was popular out-side the prison walls, too. In 1820, Robert Mackey, the first known English racquets champion, made no bones about the fact that he had learned the sport while a prisoner in Fleet Street Gaol.

Despite its lowly origins, racquets was taken up by the wealthy, who built lavish indoor courts and made the game almost their exclusive property. Then it was adopted by students at Harrow and other private schools. They added walls to the courts, im-proved the wooden paddles used, and rewrote the rules. Racquets is a mixture of jai-alai and court tennis.

Squash racquets came along shortly after racquets, but has outpaced the latter in popularity, particularly in North America. Play is in an enclosed court and a tennis-like racquet is used with a softer, hollow ball. English schoolboys, who are said to have invented the game, also are said to have given it its name because of the "squashy" sound the ball makes when it hits the court wall. At least they knew their Latin. *Squash* is from the Latin *quass*, meaning "to press flat."

Racquets and squash racquets came to the United States by way of Canada. Squash racquets, now more popular than racquets because the court is smaller and less expensive, is played in school gyms, Y's, health clubs, playgrounds, and parks around the world.

Substitute a tennis ball and a slightly different racquet and you've got yourself a game of *squash tennis*. But if you simply call a game *squash*, you're referring to squash racquets.

ROLLER SKATING

Early in the seventeenth century, a fellow in Holland got the idea of attaching wooden discs (some say spools) to his wooden shoes. He must have had a rough time of it, since streets at the time usually were paved with cobblestones.

A Belgian mechanic, Joseph Merlin, invented the first skates with metal wheels in 1763. But it wasn't until 1863 that roller skating really took off. That is the year James Leonard Plimpton, the "father of modern roller skating," introduced the *rocking skate*, which permitted the skater to steer in directions other than a straight line.

ROWING AND SCULLING

Let's get one thing straight right now. When you are in a boat and pulling on one oar, you are *rowing*. If you are pulling on two oars, you are *sculling*. The word *scull*, much used in collegiate boat races today, comes either from the French word *escouillon*, meaning "sweeper," or *escuelle*, a word for "dish." The word scull was first used in the fourteenth century to refer to the sculling oar with its dish-shaped blade.

Thomas Doggett, a London actor and comedian who died in 1715, can be credited with launching the sport of boat racing. At the time, boat traffic on the Thames River was London's principal means of transportation. Boatmen were the "taxi drivers" of the day. In his will, Doggett left a large sum of money for an annual boat race from London Bridge to Chelsea, a distance of four and one-half miles. The *Doggett Coat and Badge*, plus a sum of money, went to the winning boatman. The race is still held every year.

University students picked up on Doggett's idea and soon were staging intercollegiate boat races that developed into annual regattas attracting oarsmen from other countries, including the

United States and Canada. The *Henley Regatta* on the Thames, first held in 1839, is the world's most famous race of the sort.

The first "regatta" in America was held in 1848 in the Hudson River off Peekskill, though boat races had been reported in New York papers as early as 1811. One famous pre-American Revolution race involved a rowboat named *American Star* and used for hauling passengers. Partly because of its sleek design, the boat became the racing champ of New York harbor. The captain of a visiting British ship, *Hussar*, challenged *American Star* with his own ship's boat and offered a side bet of $1,000, a tremendous sum for the time.

The race was from Bedloe's Island up the Hudson to Hoboken, then back to the Battery at the lower end of Manhattan Island. *American Star* won by 400 yards as 60,000 people are said to have watched.

American Star later was used to transport the French General Lafayette around New York harbor and then was presented to him. He took it back to France to be copied by designers of French lifeboats.

SHUFFLEBOARD

Here's another old game with a variety of names — all of them having to do with the game equipment or how it is used. When first played in England, and possibly in Holland, *shuffleboard* was called *shove groat* and *slide groat* because the wooden disc that was shoved down the court looked like a big version of a thick English four-penny coin known as a groat. The Dutch also had a thick coin called a groat.

A later, more common, name was *shovel board*, a term derived from the long-handled wooden scoop used in the game. *Shovel*, by the way, comes from the Teutonic word *shove*, and you know what that means. Some believe *shuffleboard* is simply a slurring of shovel board. It may be, but it could have come from the Early English *scuff*, meaning "to brush with the hand" or "drag the feet." At least, the word *shuffle* did.

Dragging feet or not, shuffleboard was never quite banned by English kings as other sports were. But the game was considered a frivolous waste of time, and some monarchs let it be known that to play shuffleboard was to incur royal displeasure. Little wonder the game gravitated to America. But it was denounced in New

England as a gamblers' game, and in 1845, some cities went so far as to ban it.

Shuffleboard then faded out for a time. But interest in the game picked up again in the 1870s when the Pacific Orient steamship line began advertising it as an entertainment feature aboard its passenger ships sailing between England and Australia. They had the space and the smooth decks that were ideal for the game. (A shuffleboard court is fifty-two feet long.)

The game was resumed in the United States in the 1890s, but mainly for children. Then resort hotels in Florida installed shuffleboard courts. From there it moved to retirement communities and is presently popular among senior citizens.

YACHTING

The Dutch are believed to have been the first to use sailboats for sports, but it was England's King Charles II who got it on the sports pages. He returned from exile in Holland in 1660, having learned to sail there. He soon had a fleet of small Dutch *jaght* or *jaght schips* built and introduced sailing races on the Thames River. In 1661, the king and the Duke of York competed in a sailing race for a prize of 100 pounds. Guess who won.

Quiz Answers

AQUATICS: Leander swam at least two miles each way. But Lord Byron elected to swim across from Sestos to Abydos, which he later wrote was "not above a mile."

ARCHERY: 1. 6 feet. 2. 5 ½ feet. 3. 28 inches. 4. 25 inches. 5. 45 pounds. 6. 30 pounds. 7. 9.6 inches. 8. gold.

BASEBALL: *Big league* means major league baseball as well as wheeling and dealing in a big way, especially in high finance. *Bush league* is the opposite — the minor and semi-pro leagues in baseball and a small-timer in business or other endeavors. *Charley horse* was an aging nag with a gimpy gait that pulled a roller around the infield of the Chicago White Sox ballpark. The term is also applied to a muscle spasm in the leg causing a limping walk. *Diamond* means the ninety-foot square holding the bases. It also looks good on your girl's finger. *Dugout* is the slightly recessed area where players sit when not on the field. It's also a hole or cave dug for protection by soldiers in combat. *Fireball* is a fast pitch and also a name for a gung-ho person, a real go-getter. *Goose egg* is the big fat zero you get on the scoreboard or a no-run inning. It looks like what a goose lays. *Hardball* is the nickname given regular baseball to distinguish it from softball. When you make tough demands in a business deal, you're playing hardball.

BASKETBALL: 1. Minimum 74 x 42 feet; maximum 94 x 50 feet. 2. 20 to 22 ounces. 3. Center, left guard, right guard. 4. The pro game lasts four twelve-minute periods with a fifteen-minute rest at the half; amateurs play two twenty-minute halves. The pros play with the twenty-four-second clock rule; the amateurs do not. There are some minor differences. For example, amateurs can and often do play with a slightly smaller ball.

BOWLING: 1. A *Brooklyn* occurs when the ball hits into the pocket opposite the bowler's delivering hand. A left-hander hits the 1-3 pocket, a right-hander hits the 1-2 pocket. This is also called a "crossover." 2. *Dutch 200* is a game in which a bowler rolls alternate strikes and spares, scoring 200. 3. A *Jersey* hit is delivered by a right-handed bowler into the left-hand (1-2) pocket. 4. A *New York* hit is delivered by a left-hander into the right (1-3) pocket. 5. A *Turkey* is three strikes in a row (you should be so lucky). 6. A *Worcester* is a split leaving all but the 1 and 5 pins standing.

BOXING: Did you think of "knockout" for a beautiful girl? How about these: backpedal, beat a tattoo, bomber, breadbasket, canvasback, counterpunch, down and out, drop one's guard, haymaker, infighting, lower the boom, mouse, on one's toes, punch drunk, throw in the towel.

CROQUET: *To ring a bell.* In the early development of croquet a bell was attached to the final wicket. It rang when the ball went through. The player who rang the bell first obviously won the game. *To peg out.* This means to reach your goal in the game — to hit the final peg or stake.

CURLING: *Biter* is a stone that barely overlaps the outer edge of the house. *Burned rock* is a stone in motion that is touched by a sweeper's broom or foot. *Button* is the center ring of the house. *Draw weight* is the force needed to propel a stone into the house, that is, to "draw it in." *End* is the play of all stones toward one end of the curling sheet. Eight ends make up the usual game, sometimes ten in competition. *Guard* is a stone placed in front of and outside the house to protect a stone within it. *Hack* is two footholds in the ice from which curlers push off. *Hog line* is a line across the sheet twenty-one feet in front of the button. A stone must cross the hog line to remain in play. *In-turn* is the curving of a stone to the left, or inward across the body of a right-handed curler. *Out-turn* is the curving of a stone to the right of a curler. *Sheet* is the 138 x 14 foot ice surface used in curling. *Shot rock* is the stone nearest the center of the house, the "counter." Take-out is the act of using your own stone to knock an opponent's stone out of the house. *Tee line* is a line running across the sheet through the center of the house. *Wick* is a stone's movement to the left or right after it strikes another stone.

FENCING: Hamlet dueled with Laertes, brother of Ophelia. In *The Rivals*, Bob Acres duels with Ensign Beverly, alias Captain Absolute, over the affections of Lydia Languish.

FOOTBALL: *Boarding* — ice hockey, polo. *Charging* — basketball, field and ice hockey, football, lacrosse, rugby. *Crease* — cricket, ice hockey, lacrosse. *Dribble* — basketball, field and ice hockey, rugby, volleyball, water polo. *Hack* — curling, basketball. *Hat trick* — ice hockey, also any sport in which a player scores three times in a single game. *Interference* — football. *Jockeying* — horse racing. *Kick-off* — football, rugby. *Kill a penalty* — ice hockey. *Open net* — field and ice hockey, soccer. *Offside* — field and ice hockey, lacrosse, rugby, volleyball. *Penalty box* — ice hockey, lacrosse. *Pitch* — baseball, bowling, cricket, softball. *Pyramid* — gymnastics. *Scissors kick* — swimming. *Sweeper* — canoeing, curling, football, ice hockey, rowing, wrestling.

GOLF: *Albatross* — a double eagle. *Bird dog* — a good, alert caddie. *Birdie* — one under par for a hole. *Buzzard* — in pro slang, one over par for a hole. *Eagle* — two under par for a hole. *Double eagle* — three under par for a hole. *Quail high* — a very low drive. *Round robin* — competition in which all players are pitted against each other.

GYMNASTICS: 1. long horse, uneven bars, horizontal beam. 2. uneven bars, horizontal beam.

HANDBALL: Team and field handball are played on open grassy areas with netted goals similar to those used for soccer. Seven players usually make up a side in team handball. Up to eleven players make up a side in field handball.

HOCKEY: A goal scored "upstairs" means the puck went over the goalie's shoulder into the top of the net. Same meaning for top shelf and toy department.

LACROSSE: The sport with rules similar to lacrosse is ice hockey, though the equipment and playing areas are different. The hockey players wear ice skates, of course, while lacrosse players wear shoes with composition or rubber soles, which have studs but no spikes.

SKIING: *Alpine* and *Nordic* are the two types of competitive skiing. Alpine includes downhill, slalom, and giant slalom races. Nordic includes cross-country races and ski jumping.

SOFTBALL: 1. The ball is pitched 46 feet in both games, but for *slow pitch*, in most leagues, the ball must be lofted at least six feet above the ground. Some leagues say it must be three feet above the ground when it leaves the pitcher's hand. 2. 34 inches. 3. Fast pitch — 11 7/8 to 12 1/8 inches. Slow pitch — 14 to 16 inches. 4. Seven innings.

TENNIS: 1. 78 feet long, 27 feet wide. 2. 78 feet long, 36 feet wide. 3. Alley. 4. Three feet. 5. 3 1/2 feet. 6. 21 feet.

TABLE TENNIS: Table tennis players may not wear white clothing. White makes it hard to see the ball coming.

TRACK AND FIELD: Roger Bannister of England ran the mile in 3:59.4 minutes in 1954. We still remember him because he was first to break the four-minute mile. But do you remember John Landy? He ran a 3:58 mile only one month after Bannister made headlines.

VOLLEYBALL: Here's why volleyball is just what the doctor ordered. If the net is kept at the regulation height and a two-handed return is used, playing volleyball keeps the head and shoulders up and back, the spine straight, and the chest out — thus helping to correct "student stoop."

WRESTLING: The regulation amateur wrestling surface is a circle. It has a "central wrestling area" that is twenty-two feet wide. This is surrounded by another circle a little more than three feet wide, which is called the "passivity zone." The whole is enclosed in a square, providing a safety area extending about five feet beyond the circular mat.

Index